British Railways
The First 25 Years

Volume 10
Mid-Wales and the Cambrian Coast

including

The Central Wales Line and the Vale of Rheidol and Welshpool & Llanfair narrow gauge lines

With 2,927ft Cader Idris in the background, a boat full of tourists arrives back from a trip across the estuary and they disembark as '43XX' 2-6-0 No. 6367 comes off the bridge in July 1957. It was built in October 1925 although originally intended to be completed in 1923. This meant that it entered service with outside steam pipes, which most of the early members of the class received from the early 1930s onwards. No. 6367 was at Chester Western Region shed from July 1954 until December 1957 when it moved to Worcester. The low hump behind the viaduct is Fegla Fawr, while the higher ground on the left is 1,256ft Bryn Brith.

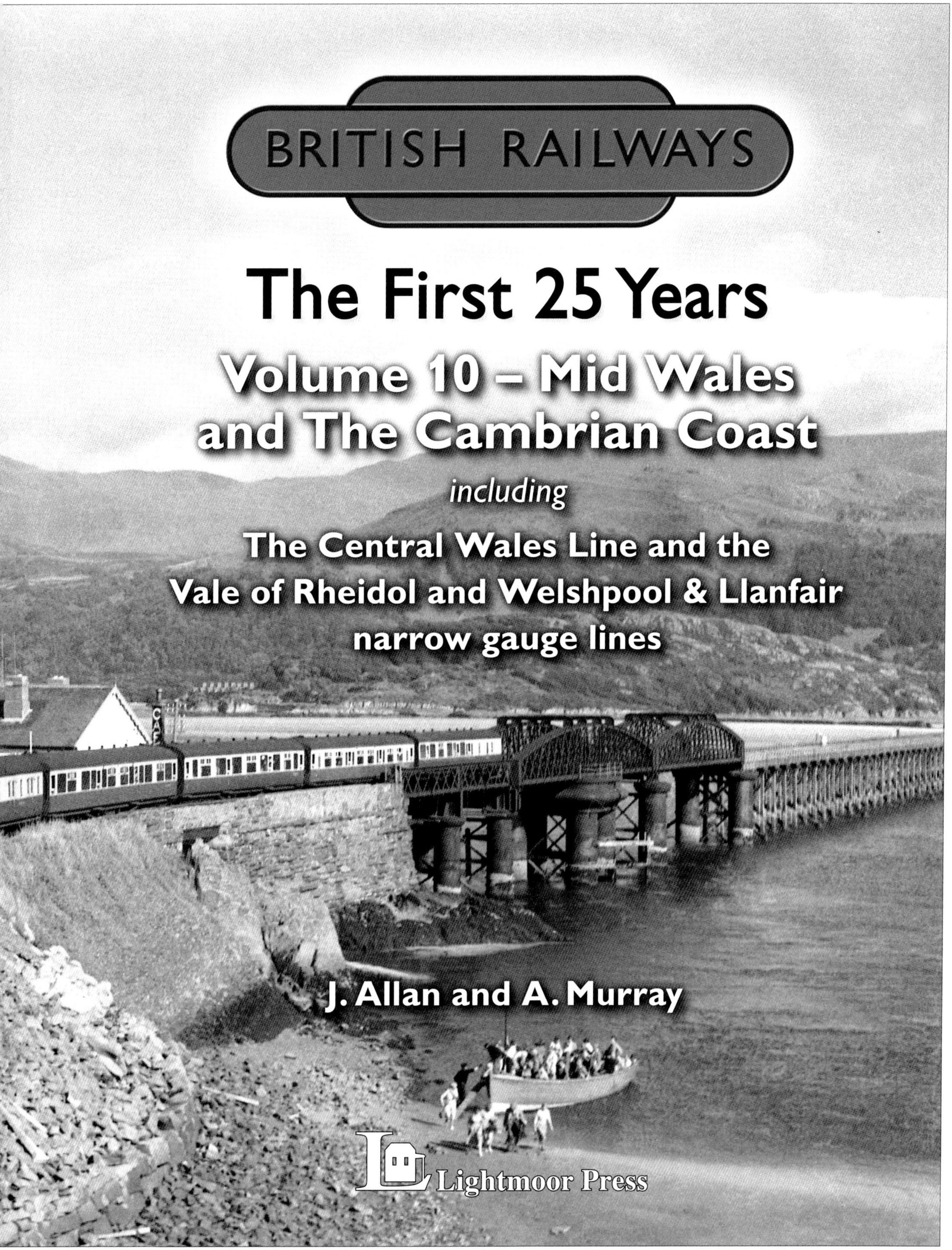

BRITISH RAILWAYS

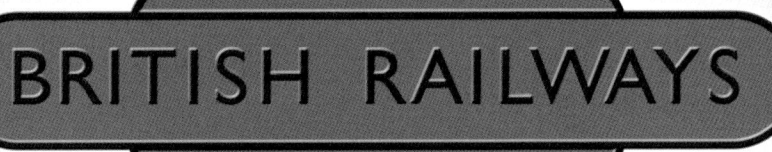

The First 25 Years

Volume 10 – Mid Wales and The Cambrian Coast

including

The Central Wales Line and the Vale of Rheidol and Welshpool & Llanfair narrow gauge lines

J. Allan and A. Murray

Lightmoor Press

Above: Churchward '43XX' 2-6-0 No. 6301 arrives at Barmouth station on 30th June 1962; another '43XX' is in the Up Bay platform on the left. The train has come from Chester via Ruabon and is bound for Pwllheli. No. 6301 was built in December 1920 and had just been transferred from Oxley to Croes Newydd; it was withdrawn in October 1962. Note the Crosville road coaches in the promenade car park on the right.

Cover photographs

Front upper: Vale of Rheidol 2-6-2T No. 7 *Owain Glyndŵr* in GWR-style lined green with matching 'chocolate and cream' coaches at Aberystwyth on 29th July 1961. The narrow gauge station was alongside the main line station, the awnings of which are visible above the coaches.

Front lower: The Eisteddfod banners and flags are out at Llangollen station as Churchward '43XX' 2-6-0 No. 5399 is about to leave with an eastbound train in July 1960. The 1920-built 'Mogul' had been at the Chester Western Region shed until April 1960 when it moved to the nearby London Midland Region depot after that shed closed.

Back upper: '90XX' 4-4-0 No. 9017 runs past the goods shed at Welshpool on 6th June 1956. The class were the principal passenger engines on the former Cambrian Railways' lines for almost two decades until the early 1950s. After withdrawal in October 1960, No. 9017 was purchased for preservation and has operated for many years on the Bluebell Railway where it runs with its original number of 3217 and the name *Earl of Berkeley* which was allocated by the GWR but never carried.

Back centre: Moat Lane Junction was where the line from Whitchurch and Oswestry to Dovey Junction and the coast met the Mid-Wales line from Three Cocks Junction and Llanidloes. Ivatt Class '2' 2-6-0 No. 46511 waits there in 1961 with a train to Brecon. This was one of twenty-five of the class built at Swindon in 1952/3 for the Western Region to replace the ageing 'Dean Goods' and Cambrian Railways' 0-6-0s on the mid-Wales services.

Back lower: The 'Cambrian Land Cruise' in typical Welsh August weather in 1958, passing an almost deserted beach at Black Rock and Tremadoc Bay. The BR Standard Class '4' 4-6-0 heads westwards on a rising gradient, which was at its steepest 1 in 82, before Criccieth was reached just a mile or so ahead. Ivatt Class '2' 2-6-0s and Collett '2251' 0-6-0s worked the circular 'Land Cruise' trains in North Wales each year until 1956, after which BR Standard Class '4' 4-6-0s took over following the raising of the route restriction from 'Yellow' to 'Blue' between Dovey Junction and Barmouth and along the coast. The stock used on these trains was an eclectic mix and the first vehicle in this formation is ex-L&NWR saloon No. 813.

© Lightmoor Press, J. Allan, A. Murray, 2020.
Designed by Stephen Phillips.

British Library Cataloguing-in-Publication Data.
A catalogue record for this book is available from the British Library.
ISBN 978-1-911038-78-8

All rights reserved. No part of this publication may be reproduced, stored in a retrieval system or transmitted in any form or by any means, electronic, mechanical, photocopying, recording or otherwise, without the written permission of the publisher.

LIGHTMOOR PRESS
Unit 144B, Lydney Trading Estate, Harbour Road,
Lydney, Gloucestershire GL15 4EJ
www.lightmoor.co.uk

Lightmoor Press is an imprint of
Black Dwarf Lightmoor Publications Ltd.

Printed in Poland
www.lfbookservices.co.uk

Contents

Introduction and Acknowledgements	7

1 Ruabon to Bala Junction   8
- Ruabon   8
- Llangollen   10
- Berwyn   13
- Corwen   14
- Bala Junction   15

2 Bala Junction to Blaenau Ffestiniog   17
- Bala   17
- Frongoch   18
- Arenig   20
- Trawsfynydd   21
- Llan Ffestiniog   22
- Blaenau Ffestiniog Central   22

3 Bala Junction to Barmouth Junction (Morfa Mawddach)   25
- Llanuwchllyn   25
- Drws-y-Nant   26
- Bontnewydd   27
- Dolgelley   28
- Penmaenpool   30
- Morfa Mawddach (Barmouth Junction)   32

4 Morfa Mawddach (Barmouth Junction) to Pwllheli   38
- Barmouth   38
- Dyffryn Ardudwy   58
- Harlech   59
- Penrhyndeudraeth   62
- Minffordd   64
- Portmadoc   69
- Black Rock   79
- Criccieth   80
- Afon Wen   83
- Penychain   87
- Pwllheli   88

5 Barmouth Junction to Dovey Junction   89
- Fairbourne   89
- Llwyngwril   90
- Towyn   92
- Aberdovey   96
- Gogarth Halt   97
- Dovey Junction   98

6 Dovey Junction to Aberystwyth   104
- Glandyfi   104
- Ynyslas   105
- Borth   106
- Aberystwyth   109

7 Vale of Rheidol Light Railway   118
- Aberystwyth   118
- Llanbadarn   123
- Aberffrwd   124
- Climbing to Devil's Bridge   124
- Devil's Bridge   127

8 Dovey Junction to Moat Lane Junction   130
- Machynlleth   130
- Cemmes Road   136
- Commins Coch   137
- Llanbrynmair   138
- Talerddig   140
- Caersws   143
- Moat Lane Junction   145

9 The Mid-Wales line: Moat Lane Junction to Three Cocks Junction   148
- Moat Lane Junction   148
- Llanidloes   149
- Tylwch Halt   150
- Pantydwr   151
- Rhayader   151
- Newbridge on Wye   153
- Doldowlod   153
- Builth Road (Low Level)   154
- Builth Wells   155
- Erwood   157
- Llanstephan Halt   159
- Boughrood & Llyswen   160
- Three Cocks Junction   160

10 The Central Wales line   163
- Craven Arms and Stokesay   164
- Broome   165
- Knighton   166
- Pen-y-Bont   167
- Llandrindod Wells   167
- Builth Road (High Level)   168
- Llanwrtyd Wells   170
- Sugar Loaf Summit   171
- Cynghordy   172
- Llandovery   174

11 Moat Lane Junction to Welshpool   177
- Newtown   177
- Abermule   178
- Forden   178
- Welshpool   179

12 Welshpool & Llanfair Light Railway   185
- Welshpool   185
- Llanfair Caereinion   189
- Castle Caereinion   189
- Seven Stars   190
- Buttington   191

13 Welshpool to Oswestry   191
- Four Crosses   193
- Llanymynech   194
- The Llanfyllin branch   196
- Llynclys   198

14 Oswestry   199
- Stations   199
- Oswestry shed   205
- Oswestry Works   208

BR Standard Class '3' 2-6-2T No. 82020 on a Pwllheli-Dovey Junction service at Portmadoc in 1963. It was at Machynlleth from March 1960 until April 1965 when it went to the Southern Region at Nine Elms for use on the Waterloo Empty Coaching Stock work. No. 82020 had been repainted from its original lined black livery into lined green at Swindon Works in 1958, but lost the lining at its next repaint in July 1961.

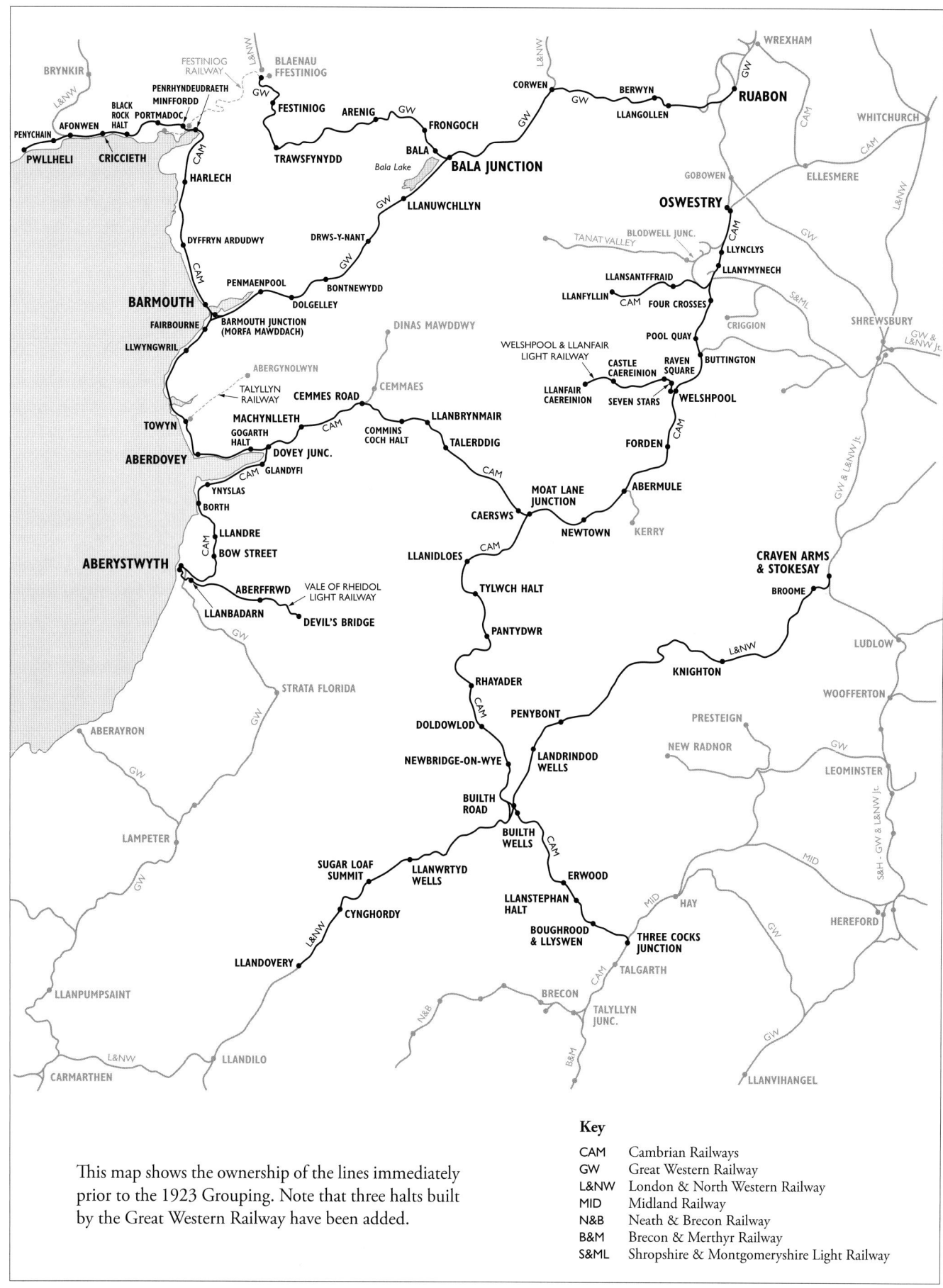

This map shows the ownership of the lines immediately prior to the 1923 Grouping. Note that three halts built by the Great Western Railway have been added.

Key

CAM	Cambrian Railways
GW	Great Western Railway
L&NW	London & North Western Railway
MID	Midland Railway
N&B	Neath & Brecon Railway
B&M	Brecon & Merthyr Railway
S&ML	Shropshire & Montgomeryshire Light Railway

Introduction and Acknowledgements

This is the tenth in a series of books depicting the first twenty-five years of British Railways, and which will eventually cover the whole of the UK. This volume covers the lines in mid-Wales, from Oswestry out to the Cambrian Coast. We have kept the English spelling of place names which were in use during most of the period rather than the later Welsh versions, except for photographs taken after the names officially changed. The history of much of the railway in this area was complex and although eventually in 1923 most of the lines except for the Central Wales line came under Great Western Railway control, they were built piecemeal by smaller local companies. Until the Grouping, the only GWR line in Mid-Wales was from Ruabon along the Dee Valley to Dolgelley and the branch to Blaenau Ffestiniog; the remainder eventually became part of the Cambrian Railways. In each chapter we have summarised the contribution from the original companies but have left discussion of the detailed historical background to the specialised books on those lines.

We start at Ruabon following the line to Bala Junction where we divert up the Blaenau Ffestiniog Central branch before resuming our journey west towards Barmouth where the Cambrian Railways took over from the GWR at Dolgelley. Taking the fork north at Barmouth Junction (Morfa Mawddach from 1960) to Barmouth itself we go up the coast to Portmadoc and on to the terminus at Pwllheli. Returning to Barmouth Junction we turn south to Aberdovey and reach Dovey Junction where we take the line to Aberystwyth to allow a visit to the Vale of Rheidol narrow gauge line. We return to Dovey Junction and go east through Machynlleth to a third junction, at Moat Lane, and divert again, this time on to the former Mid-Wales Railway down to Three Cocks Junction. This line crossed the former London & North Western Railway Central Wales line at Builth and so we take the opportunity to cover the part of that line in mid-Wales, from Craven Arms as far south as Llandovery. Resuming our journey at Moat Lane we stop at Welshpool to visit another narrow gauge line, the Welshpool & Llanfair, before our final leg to Oswestry, pausing briefly along the way for the short branch to Llanfyllin. Oswestry was the headquarters of the Cambrian Railways and we end with a visit to its depot and works.

With the exception of most of the Cambrian main line between Oswestry and Moat Lane Junction, these were predominantly single lines where the weekday pattern of operation was transformed every summer Saturday. The former Cambrian Railways routes pivoted around the three junctions of Moat Lane Junction, Dovey Junction and Barmouth Junction. The first two were built purely to inter-change passengers between the lines which met there and were almost inaccessible except by the railway.

In the first few years after nationalisation Cambrian Railways' Class '15' 0-6-0s and Great Western Railway 'Dean Goods' 0-6-0s, '43XX' 2-6-0s, '2251' 0-6-0s ,'45XX' 2-6-2Ts and 'Earl' (90XX) 4-4-0s (nicknamed 'Dukedogs' by enthusiasts from the early 1950s) continued to work over these lines. In the early 1950s newly built LM&SR Ivatt Class '2' 2-6-0s and their BR Standard equivalent '78XXX' 2-6-0s took over many of their duties. In 1943 the first 'Manor' class 4-6-0s arrived and were joined in the 1950s by BR '75XXX' Class '4' 4-6-0s; they replaced the '43XX' 2-6-0s and the '90XX' 4-4-0s on the principal passenger services. Finally, in the early 1960s the last GWR engines were ousted as more BR Standard classes arrived after they were displaced elsewhere. On the Central Wales line, despite its transfer to Western Region control in 1948, change came slower with the pre-war allocations of Fowler 2-6-4Ts, Stanier Class '5' 4-6-0s and even 'Jubilee' 4-6-0s working the Shrewsbury-Swansea passenger services until 1964 with L&NWR 0-8-0s and '8F' 2-8-0s handling the freight traffic.

At nationalisation, all of the lines in this volume came under the Western Region of British Railways. The first to close, except for the Welshpool and Llanfair, was the Mid-Wales line in late 1962. On 1st January 1963 the remaining ex-Cambrian lines were transferred to the London Midland Region. In January 1965, the Ruabon-Barmouth line was closed and the Cambrian passenger services between Whitchurch and Welshpool were withdrawn. Only a handful of diesel multiple units and diesel locomotives feature because most of the lines covered here closed with the end of steam; only the route from Welshpool to Aberystwyth and to Pwllheli survived the Beeching 'Axe'.

Acknowledgements

Once again, we are grateful for the expertise and enthusiasm of Steve Phillips who designed this book and helped with the captions for the Vale of Rheidol chapter. Our thanks also go to Vic Smith, Martin Brown, Andrew Dyke, Derek Lowe and Martin Williams for their comments and corrections. Any errors remaining are of course entirely the responsibility of the authors and publishers.

The majority of the pictures in this volume are from the Rail-Online.co.uk collection with many from Rail Archive Stephenson. We have taken the opportunity to include over fifty whole page portraits which bring out the quality of these fifty or sixty-year old photographs.

References

We have used a number of books to provide details of locomotives and workings and in particular the RCTS *BR Standard* and *Great Western* series and the Irwell Press *Book of* series. *The Welshpool & Llanfair Light Railway* by R. Cartwright and R.T. Russell, *Shrewsbury to Swansea* by D.J. Smith and C.C. Green's *The Coast Lines of the Cambrian Railways* were consulted for historical background as were several other Lightmoor Press books – *The Bala Branch*, *The Ruabon to Barmouth Line* and *Cambrian Diary*.

J. Allan
A. Murray

1 – Ruabon to Bala Junction

The Great Western line from Ruabon to Bala was built by three different but connected companies, supported by the GWR which operated the line from the start. These were the Vale of Llangollen Railway (Ruabon to Llangollen completed in 1861), the Llangollen & Corwen Railway (opened in May 1865), and the Corwen & Bala Railway (completed in 1868); all three were absorbed by the Great Western in 1896.

Until the summer of 1927, the line was classed as 'uncoloured', which restricted the type of locomotives which were permitted to haul trains to the coast at Barmouth. The track was renewed and bridges were strengthened or replaced to allow locomotives with an axle weight up to 17tons 12cwt. This now became a 'blue' route allowing classes such as the '43XX' 2-6-0s and '57XX' panniers and, later, 'Manor' 4-6-0s to work over the line.

Passenger services were withdrawn between Ruabon and Bala in January 1965, but freight continued between Ruabon and Llangollen until April 1968.

Ruabon

Ruabon was the junction with the Great Western's Chester-Shrewsbury main line and by the early 1900s the facilities there needed to be improved to cater for the increased traffic levels. New platforms were constructed, a bay platform added for the Barmouth trains and the original footbridge was replaced.

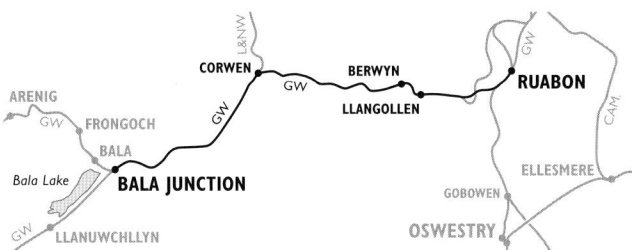

Churchward '43XX' 2-6-0 No. 5399 at Ruabon working a train to Barmouth and Pwllheli, probably in 1957. Summer Saturday trains to the coast were frequently double-headed; in this case the 'Mogul' is working with a Collett '2251' 0-6-0. No. 5399 was built in November 1920 and had outside steam pipes when new cylinders were fitted in February 1957, one of the last of the class to be modified in this way. It was allocated to the former Great Western shed at Chester from October 1955 until April 1960 when it moved to the Chester London Midland Region shed when the GWR shed closed.

One of the typical GWR large running-in boards at its junction stations reads 'RUABON JUNCTION FOR LLANGOLLEN CORWEN BALA FESTINIOG DOLGELLEY & BARMOUTH'. To the right of this, visible under the footbridge is the former refreshment room building, used by this time as a railwaymens' social club. The line to the right once served a cattle dock beyond the bay platform.

An Ivatt Class '2' 2-6-0 waits in the bay platform with a local for the Barmouth line on 24th August 1963. In the background is the large goods shed and the sidings which until the late 1960s handled a large volume of coal traffic from the local collieries which produced coal suitable for domestic use. *Robert Darlaston*

BR Standard Class '4' 2-6-4T No. 80078 in the Barmouth bay at Ruabon with the 11.0am SO to Barmouth on 24th August 1963. A former London, Tilbury & Southend line engine ousted by electrification, it arrived at Shrewsbury in July 1962 and moved to Croes Newydd in February 1963. After withdrawal in July 1965 it was rescued from Woodhams scrapyard at Barry by the Southern Steam Trust. No. 80078 was sold to a group of individuals in 1991 and restored in the Southern Locomotives Ltd programme for use on the Swanage Railway where it worked in the early 21st century. It was purchased privately in 2012 and has worked on several heritage lines since. Note the other running-in board advising passengers that this was 'RUABON JUNCTION FOR CHESTER & THE NORTH SHREWSBURY & THE SOUTH'. *Robert Darlaston*

Llangollen

The station at Llangollen had to fit into the restricted space available as the line followed the River Dee. It was enlarged in 1898 when the line from Ruabon was doubled and there were now two platforms, curved in an elongated 'S' shape. The main building was also extended, and a footbridge added. Ten years after closure of the line in 1965, the Flint & Deeside Railway Preservation Society re-opened the station on 13th September 1975, with just sixty feet of track, after the local council granted a lease of the Llangollen station building and three miles of the trackbed towards Berwyn. The Preservation Society was wound up in 1977 and its assets transferred to the Llangollen Railway Society. Almost three decades later, in 2014, the Llangollen Railway was re-opened to Corwen having been reinstated in stages over those intervening years.

The 'Eisteddfod Llangollen 1960' banner (to the right of the signal box in this picture) and bunting decorate the station as passengers stream off the train which had arrived behind Churchward '43XX' 2-6-0 No. 5322. The international music festival began in 1947 and took place every July, attracting significant additional traffic to the town over the two-week duration. No. 5322 was one of eleven '43XX' built at Swindon in 1917 which were sent when new to the War Department for operation in France and returned safely to the GWR in 1919. It was renumbered as 8322 in 1928 when modified with a casting behind the front buffer beam to reduce flange wear on the leading coupled wheels. This was removed in 1944 and it reverted to No. 5322; outside steam pipes and new cylinders were fitted in October 1949. No. 5322 was allocated to Pontypool Road from September 1959 until withdrawn in April 1964 when it went to Woodham Brothers scrapyard. Fortunately, as the only surviving early '43XX', it was acquired by a Great Western Society member in 1969, the first ex-GWR locomotive to leave the scrapyard for preservation. However, it was not restored for many years, but after the Society took over its ownership it was eventually returned to traffic in November 2008, restored to its 1919 R.O.D. condition. No. 5322 was withdrawn in Summer 2014 with cracks in its firebox and has not been steamed since. In the distance beyond the footbridge is a large water tank which supplied three water-columns on the platforms, two on the Down side serving local and excursion trains and one on the Up side.

Churchward '43XX' 2-6-0 No. 5385 has just left Llangollen with an eastbound freight in July 1960. It was allocated to St. Philip's Marsh shed at Bristol from September 1958 until June 1962. The train is in the Vale of Llangollen where the line ran between the Shropshire Union Canal to the right and the River Dee on the left. The make-up of the train with nine 'Presflo' cement hoppers and a couple of tank wagons behind is interesting. The cement wagons were probably empties returning from the Blaenau Ffestiniog branch in connection with the construction of the Trawsfynydd nuclear power station which had started in 1959.

In this picture taken from the river bridge, a westbound train full of visitors to the Eisteddfod headed by '43XX' 2-6-0 No. 7314 approaches the station in July 1957. No. 7314 was built at Swindon in December 1921 and had been allocated to Llanelly since April 1956. Note the floodlights to illuminate the bridge over the River Dee.

'43XX' 2-6-0 No. 6357 runs alongside the River Dee at Llangollen with a four-coach 'Ordinary Passenger Train' from Ruabon in 1959. Built in November 1923 and fitted with outside steam pipes in 1953, it had been transferred from Tyseley to Croes Newydd in April 1959 and was there until January 1962 when it moved west to Carmarthen. To the left of the train is the short siding once used by 'assisting engines' to help heavy trains on the climb up to Ruabon where there was a continuous gradient of almost four miles at between 1 in 74 and 1 in 87.

As his fireman fills up the tanks, the driver of '74XX' 0-6-0PT No. 7414 on a Bala to Ruabon pick-up goods climbs up the steps of Llangollen Station Signal Box on 21st July 1962. The '74XX' was a small-wheeled version of the '54XX' which was itself a light passenger version of the '57XX' pannier. They were not auto-fitted and had 180lb rather than 165lb boiler pressure and lever reverse which made them ideal for freight and shunting work. No. 7414 was allocated to Croes Newydd from 1941 until April 1963. The twenty-five lever signal box on the Up platform, dating from 1898, was usually switched-out and only opened when required; behind it was a small loading bay. The footbridge from the main building crossed the line and, because of the restricted space and to conform to minimum platform width regulations, the steps on the Down side had to overhang the river.

Berwyn

With the River Dee on the left, '57XX' 0-6-0PT No. 8791 departs from Berwyn on a Ruabon-Barmouth train in around 1957. The pannier was allocated to Croes Newydd from August 1956 until May 1961 when it went to Hereford. The rear of the train is on the six arch viaduct, which at one time was fitted with steel supports for the extension to the platform visible to the right of the train (removed in around 1960). Each arch was of a different width, varying from 29ft 9in. to 30ft 3in. The viaduct was thirty-six feet above the Eirianallt stream and there were major earthworks and stone abutments on both sides of it. The suspension bridge over the River Dee is just visible through the trees on the left. There was a permanent 25mph speed restriction through the station because of the curves, which surprisingly did not have a check rail. The single platform (with its later extension) was 359ft long. The station was constructed in a 'mock Tudor' style, as can be glimpsed at the rear of the train, and contained residential accommodation in the upper part of the building in addition to the usual booking office, waiting rooms, etc.

Corwen

At Corwen the Ruabon-Bala line had a junction with the line built by the Denbigh, Ruthin & Corwen Railway which ran south along the valley of the River Clwyd. The latter was operated by the L&NWR and reached Corwen late in 1864 a few months before the Llangollen & Corwen Railway arrived there in May 1865. The two lines met east of the town and they used a temporary station until the permanent one was built. Corwen was viewed by both companies as an important railway centre in this part of Wales and it became the largest intermediate station on the Ruabon to Barmouth line. Extensive sidings were constructed, as well as goods facilities, together with a jointly owned locomotive shed. Westwards, the Corwen & Bala Railway was completed in 1868. The line was built in two sections, firstly to Llandrillo, which opened in July 1866 and then the second stage to Bala in April 1868.

BR Standard Class '4' 4-6-0 No. 75029 waits for the signal at Corwen with a train for Chester in 1963. It has a 6C Croes Newydd shed plate and had been transferred from Machynlleth to the Wrexham shed in November 1962; it was there until June 1965. In May 1957 No. 75029 was the first of nine engines in the class to be fitted with a double blastpipe chimney to improve the efficiency of its draughting and at the same visit to Swindon Works was the first of the class to be repainted in lined green livery. Fittingly, after purchase for preservation by the famous railway and wildlife artist David Shepherd it was given the name *The Green Knight*. On the left is the setting-down post for the single line token; these were rarely used, the engine crew normally giving the signalmen the tokens at the station platform.

Another view on the same day of BR Standard Class '4' 4-6-0 No. 75029 showing the eastern end of Corwen. The expensive to maintain scissors crossover was needed because the tracks in front of the train are not double track but were for two separate routes which divided a few hundred yards away from the platform. On the left is the ex-L&NWR line to Ruthin which had been closed in April 1962, having lost its passenger service in 1953; the one on the right is the GWR line to Ruabon.

Bala Junction

Bala Junction was where the Blaenau Ffestiniog branch joined the Ruabon-Dolgelly line. When opened in 1882, the station was in the middle of fields and was not included in the public timetables of the GWR or in Bradshaw. It was purely an interchange station with no road access, although after the 1923 grouping it could be reached by a public footpath.

Above: Churchward '43XX' 2-6-0 No. 6311 at Bala Junction coming off the Blaenau line in June 1956. No. 6311 was at Croes Newydd for nine years, from late 1949 until transferred to Oxley in October 1958. Although the line between Bala to Trawsfynydd was upgraded from a 'yellow' to a 'blue' route to allow larger engines such as '43XX' 2-6-0s to haul army traffic to the camp at Trawsfynydd, these were almost unknown in peacetime. They could not travel beyond Trawsfynydd to Blaenau and had to return down the branch tender-first which suggests that No. 6311 had only worked its train over the short 55 chains distance from the large goods yard and depot at Bala having reversed there to collect wagons from the yard. The empty tank wagons would have been picked up from the petrol depot at Dolgelley. Note the spelling of Festiniog on the running-in board – the boards at the terminus had been changed to Ffestiniog in 1951.

Left: BR Standard Class '4' 4-6-0 No. 75028 arriving with the 12.45pm Pwllheli to Chester on 11th June 1959. It went from Oswestry to Chester West in September 1958 and then to Rhyl in June 1959 but was only there for three months, returning to Chester West. The line to Bala and Blaenau curves away to the right; the hill in the background is Arenig Fawr which rises to a height of 2,802ft.

The staple motive power on the Blaenau Ffestiniog branch during its final decade were pannier tanks, mostly the ubiquitous '57XX' but also the '74XX' class. '57XX' No. 4645 waits in the branch platform at Bala Junction with the 2.20pm from Blaenau Ffestiniog on 15th September 1958. It was allocated to Croes Newydd from October 1950 until withdrawn in November 1965.
Robert Darlaston

Passenger traffic ceased on the Blaenau Ffestiniog branch on 2nd January 1960 to allow construction work to begin on the dam in the Tryweryn valley although a service continued from Bala to Bala Junction to connect with the Ruabon to Barmouth line services as well as through trains from Bala to Wrexham and Birkenhead. The pannier tanks were transferred away and were replaced by Ivatt Class '2' 2-6-0s, one of which No. 46509, waits to leave the branch platform at Bala Junction with the single coach 'shuttle' to Bala on 23rd July 1963. Behind the train is Bala Junction Signal Box, the largest intermediate signal box on the Ruabon-Barmouth line.
Brian Stephenson

2 – Bala Junction to Blaenau Ffestiniog

In 1862 the Festiniog & Blaenau Railway was formed to build a narrow gauge line from Ffestiniog to Blaenau Ffestiniog to convey slate from the numerous slate mines in and around Blaenau Ffestiniog and to connect with the already established Festiniog Railway from Portmadoc. The Festiniog & Blaenau Railway opened to traffic in May 1868 with the same gauge of 1ft 11½in. as the Festiniog Railway. In November 1882 the Bala & Festiniog Railway opened a standard gauge railway from a point on the Ruabon-Barmouth line (later Bala Junction) to Festiniog. At Festiniog, slate was transferred from the narrow gauge wagons of the Festiniog & Blaenau onto standard gauge wagons, an expensive operation both in time and labour. The Bala & Festiniog Railway jointly with the Great Western Railway purchased the narrow gauge line in April 1883 and by September the line had been converted to standard gauge enabling trains to run through from Bala to Blaenau Ffestiniog, a distance of 25½ miles. The GWR worked the line from the outset but did not take over the Bala & Festiniog until 1910. The railway climbed up from Bala to 1,278 feet above sea level near Cwm Prysor, almost halfway along the line, before descending back down to Blaenau Ffestiniog. The line was not only severely graded with many sections at 1 in 50 but had many sharp curves, resulting in a maximum allowed speed of 45mph.

In the early 1950s, the GWR classes used in the post-war years continued to work the branch, '74XX' 0-6-0PTs, '58XX' 0-4-2Ts and '2251' 0-6-0s. The latter were apparently popular with the engine crews but they tended to slip badly on the many sharp curves and were replaced once the '57XX' panniers were cleared to run on the line; the less powerful 0-4-2Ts had also disappeared by the mid-1950s. All of the engines were supplied from Croes Newydd shed at Wrexham; none were auto-fitted.

In 1957 Liverpool Corporation obtained authorisation to build a dam and reservoir in the Tryweryn valley. This would mean flooding a section of the branch near to Tyddyn Bridge Halt and the British Transport Commission drew up plans to deviate the line, but it was soon decided that the cost did not justify the benefits of retaining the railway and it would be closed. Although there was considerable local opposition to the closure, as well as to the dam project itself, this was in vain and passenger traffic ceased in January 1960. A shuttle service between Bala and Bala Junction was retained to connect with the Ruabon to Barmouth line services and through trains from Bala to Wrexham and Birkenhead continued. Freight services lasted for another year, but they too ended in January 1961.

This was not quite the end of the story because, as part of the arrangement, Liverpool Corporation funded the construction of a connection between the Western Region and the London Midland Region stations at Blaenau. This was opened in April 1964 to allow for the future transportation of nuclear waste from Trawsfynydd to Sellafield; it was mothballed after the power station was decommissioned and the last train ran in 1997.

Bala

'57XX' 0-6-0PT No. 8791 at Bala with the usual single coach train to Blaenau Ffestiniog in around 1958. After it was transferred to Croes Newydd in August 1956 No. 8791 was a regular on the branch until closure. Bala Station was only 55 chains down the line from Bala Junction and had two platforms. There was also a large goods yard and sidings which could handle up to one hundred wagons, and a small engine shed.

Frongoch

Pannier tank No. 9793 simmers in the sunshine at Frongoch on the 2.20pm Blaenau Ffestiniog-Bala Junction in August 1958 while the guard and footplate crew chew the cud with the signalman/porter and station master on the otherwise deserted platform. Opposite Frongoch Signal Box is the 'picking-up' post for the staff section to Arenig, complete with its lamp, which was probably seldom used. Frongoch, the first station out of Bala, was 3 miles 23 chains from Bala Junction. There was only one platform with a small single storey building which housed a booking office and general waiting room. Also on the platform was a typical GWR-style metal lock-up shed and a small signal box, measuring 13ft 7in. by 12ft 1in. Its frame, which housed eleven levers, five of them spare, controlled the few signals at the station as well as the points for the goods yard. The signalling instruments, however, were not in the box but in the booking office. The box was manned from 6.45am to 8.40pm but remained open until 9.25pm on Saturdays and could not be 'switched out'. Frongoch station was a 'block post' for signalling purposes but, since there was no passing loop, trains could not be crossed there. However, a goods train could be put into the siding which is just visible to the left of the rear of the train to allow another train to pass and this occurred occasionally to allow the passage of a passenger train.

CHAPTER 2 - BALA JUNCTION TO BLAENAU FFESTINIOG

Another view of No. 9793 at Frongoch in August 1958 on the 2.20pm Blaenau Ffestiniog-Bala Junction which reached Bala at 3.37pm. On weekdays in 1958 there were four trains in each direction, taking approximately an hour and a half for the journey. Built in June 1936, No. 9793 was the later '8750' version of the '57XX' pannier tank with improved cabs which had a more rounded roof profile, sliding shutters and larger front windows. From 1950 the route availability of the class was changed from 'blue' to 'yellow' after their hammer blow was re-assessed, allowing their use on the branch. No. 9793 moved from Tyseley to Croes Newydd in June 1951 and remained there until withdrawn in August 1963.

Arenig

The Stephenson Locomotive Society organised a special train from Ruabon to Blaenau Ffestiniog and return to bid farewell to the line on Sunday 22nd January 1961. British Railways arranged for eight coaches to be stabled in the bay platform at Ruabon for the trip and they were collected by two specially prepared Croes Newydd pannier tanks, Nos. 4645 and 8791. The BBC recorded it for their 'Railway Roundabout' television series, travelling on the train and along the road to record the journey. The special pauses at Arenig where photographers climbed signal ladders and every available vantage point to photograph the train whilst the engines took on water. In the quarry line on the left a loaded hopper wagon waits ready for collection in the coming days before the line was finally severed on 28th January.

Another view of the SLS special at Arenig viewed from track level. The fireman of pannier tank No. 4645 is standing on the engine checking the water level as the tanks are replenished.
Robert Darlaston

Trawsfynydd

A train for Bala, headed by pannier tank No. 9793, pauses at Trawsfynydd in August 1958 and the crew take the opportunity to replenish the tanks of the engine. In the distance beyond the over-bridge, part of the military sidings is visible. Trawsfynydd was the largest intermediate station on the line and was about half a mile from the village it served. In 1903 the British Army opened a camp for training purposes south of the village which was used extensively by the regular Army and Territorials and the troops, horses, gun carriages and supplies would arrive by train due to the poor local roads. It soon became apparent that the facilities at the station needed improvement to handle the increasing traffic and in 1910 construction started on a separate station purely for military use north of the existing passenger station. At the same time, the latter was upgraded with new platforms, new signalling and a replacement signal box of standard GWR design which controlled the station area as well as access into the military sidings. Military traffic reduced after the war ended in 1945 apart from a period when large quantities of unused ammunition were brought in by train for destruction; the camp was eventually closed in the late-1950s. Note the unusual slate-hung side of the signal box is already showing signs of neglect. Unlike Bala, no footbridge was provided, and passengers had to use the boarded crossing in the foreground.

Llan Ffestiniog

'2251' 0-6-0 No. 2259 in the late-1940s looking south towards Festiniog station about three miles south of Blaenau Ffestiniog. The Collett 0-6-0s had a tendency to slip on the many curves on the line and '57XX' pannier tanks replaced them in the early 1950s. One of two of the class shedded at Croes Newydd from pre-nationalisation days, No. 2259 remained there or at Machynlleth until autumn 1953. Festiniog, which served the village of Llan Ffestiniog, was the southern terminus for the narrow gauge Festiniog & Blaenau Railway and the original northern terminus for the line from Bala before the narrow gauge line was converted to allow the standard gauge line to continue to Blaenau Ffestiniog.

Blaenau Ffestiniog Central

'57XX' 0-6-0PT No. 9669 after arrival at Blaenau Ffestiniog with a train from Bala with another pannier beyond the signal box. No. 9669 was at Croes Newydd from new in May 1948 until May 1962 when it was transferred to Duffryn Yard. The '57XX' panniers were only allowed to work between Festiniog and Blaenau Ffestiniog if they were fitted with flange oilers due to the severe curves on this section, and they were not allowed into some of the sidings at Manod, Pengwern, Tan-y-Manod and Blaenau Ffestiniog. Behind the station building is the roof of the Queen's Hotel, which was a popular meeting place for railwaymen at the end of their shifts. The small building on the left of the picture was used as a lamp room.   *Stephen Summerson/Rail Archive Stephenson*

'74XX' 0-6-0PT No. 7433 waiting to depart from Blaenau Ffestiniog Central in the late 1950s was at Croes Newydd from new in August 1948 until withdrawn in February 1961 after the line closed. The class was used on both passenger and freight duties on the branch and one was regularly stabled overnight at Trawsfynydd. Because Blaenau station had to be built in a restricted space, there was only a single platform, and the entrance to the station building was in the gable end wall facing the approach. The Festiniog Railway station, closed in 1946, was behind and the two lines shared the 435 feet long platform. In the background is the footbridge from the town that crossed the narrow gauge line to give access to the platform for both railways. On 18th June 1951, the station was renamed Blaenau Ffestiniog (replacing the single 'f' spelling of Festiniog). As the running-in board shows they did a poor job of matching the 'F' letter style which was surprising as they were standard cast letters; it was also given the suffix 'Central' and at the same the ex-LM&SR station was similarly renamed, becoming Blaenau Ffestiniog North.

'57XX' No. 9793 at Blaenau Ffestiniog Central with the single coach Bala train in April 1958. The station originally had two signal boxes, but these were replaced in September 1926 by this GWR standard design which had thirty-one levers and the staff instruments for the section to Festiniog. Lever No. 7 in the frame blocked all movements at the far end of the layout to prevent collisions when the Festiniog Railway narrow gauge trains crossed over the standard gauge track to reach the goods yard. The small dock and loading bay off the platform line was used for livestock.

3 – Bala Junction to Barmouth Junction (Morfa Mawddach)

The Bala & Dolgelly Railway, which was operated from the outset by the Great Western Railway, completed its 17¼ miles long line to Dolgelley in August 1868 where it would meet in the following year the line from Barmouth which had been hurriedly built by as a protective measure against the GWR reaching the coast. This had been started by the Aberystwith [sic] & Welsh Coast Railway but was completed by the Cambrian Railways into which the former company was amalgamated when the latter was formed in July 1865. The Barmouth-Dolgelley line did not open until June 1869 and both companies used a temporary terminus until the new joint station opened the following year.

Until the 1923 Grouping the station at Dolgelley was operated separately, the Cambrian using the Down platform and the GWR the Up platform, and each had its own staff and station master. Although the GWR had running powers to Barmouth, the two companies treated Dolgelley predominantly as the terminus of their respective lines. After 1923 the trains from Ruabon worked through to Barmouth while a shuttle service operated between Barmouth and Dolgelley. The line was closed following recommendations in the Beeching Report, in January 1965.

Llanuwchllyn

Two views of BR Standard Class '4' 4-6-0 No. 75006 at Llanuwchllyn on the 12.45pm Pwllheli-Birkenhead in August 1963. Although difficult to see in these pictures, it had green livery from December 1960 at which date it was fitted with a double chimney. No. 75006 had been transferred from Machynlleth to Croes Newydd in March 1963, remaining there until November 1964 when it left for Stoke.

Above: Each platform had a 'parachute' type water-tank to assist train workings and the water came from a small well, situated near the bridge at Garth Isaf, some 700 yards towards Garneddwen; it was piped to the tanks and gravity fed, down the gradient. Note on the left, the 'setting-down' post for the token from Bala Junction with its safety net. The 'picking up' post for the next section to Garneddwen or Drws-y-Nant was situated a few yards further on adjacent to the foot crossing.

Right:
The signal box was at the east end of the Up platform and controlled the whole station area and the single line sections to Bala Junction in the east, and to Drws-y-Nant or Garneddwen Loop in the west, it contained a twenty-one lever 'double twist' frame. The small cattle-dock, at the end of the Up platform, saw a great deal of traffic over the years. Occasionally, to save waiting, cattle were unloaded directly onto the platform rather than the cattle dock. Today, the former station is the headquarters of the 2ft gauge Bala Lake Railway which uses a 4½ mile section of the old trackbed to Bala.

BR Standard Class '4' 4-6-0 No. 75023 approaching Llanuwchllyn station on a westbound train. It was at Croes Newydd from March 1963 until January 1965 when it left for Stoke although the 89B shed plate puts the date of this picture as before September 1963 when the code became 6C under the London Midland Region. The goods yard siding at the east end of the station ran in parallel to the running lines and had a small stone-built goods shed and, beyond it, a corrugated shed which was added in later years.

Drws-y-Nant

Croes Newydd's '43XX' 2-6-0 No. 6316 working a Chester-Pwllheli Ordinary Passenger train near Drws-y-Nant on 30th July 1951. Behind, to the right are the slopes of Aran Benllyn which reach a height of 2,904 feet. The train has just crossed over the Afon Ty-cerig (a subsidiary of the Afon Winion) and a minor road which served a number of small settlements. The line on this section had to be laid on numerous small embankments and through cuttings as the railway crossed numerous rivers and streams. Only the riverside bridge abutment survives today, and although the embankment remains reasonably intact it is almost indistinguishable as it is now covered with mature trees.

The Ivatt 2-6-0s worked on the Ruabon to Barmouth line in its final years until the end in January 1965. No. 46509 drops down the Wnion Valley and approaches Drws-y-nant station with a train to Barmouth in October 1964. This was not a double track section; the long passing loop extended some way beyond the platforms.

Bontnewydd

The now-preserved BR Standard Class '4' 4-6-0 No. 75029 from Croes Newydd shed with a westbound train at Bontnewydd in 1964. The station originally had a single platform but the Great Western Railway carried out improvements in 1923, putting in a crossing loop and a second platform on the Down side, built of timber on supports because of its position on an embankment. The only building on the Down platform was the corrugated iron waiting shelter on the right of the picture, and beyond that is the signal box dating from August 1923 when it replaced an earlier box.

Dolgelley

With the Wnion river on the left, 'Manor' 4-6-0 No. 7822 *Foxcote Manor* arrives at Dolgelley with a Barmouth to Ruabon train in the late 1950s. No. 7822 had been transferred from Oswestry to Machynlleth in December 1963, staying until January 1965 when it moved to Shrewsbury from where it was withdrawn the following November. Fittingly, after its purchase from Barry scrapyard in 1972, *Foxcote Manor* has been based at the Llangollen Railway since 1985. No 7817 *Garsington Manor* which went new to Croes Newydd at Wrexham was recorded on a trial run from Oswestry to Aberystwyth in December 1940, but it was not until 1943 that any were allocated to Cambrian sheds. No. 7807 *Compton Manor* was transferred to Oswestry on 1st March 1943 and was followed two months later by No. 7819 *Hinton Manor*. They were immediately employed on passenger work between Oswestry and Aberystwyth and were a big improvement from the operating point of view, because they could climb Talerdigg bank without assistance. In their early days, the performance of the class was inferior to the '43XX' 2-6-0s which, along with the 'Grange' 4-6-0s, they were intended to replace. Although they were heavier, they had a lighter axle loading but they did not steam as well as the 'Moguls'. The Second World War put a brake on the introduction of more of the class until after nationalisation when British Railways built ten more of them in 1950/51, including No. 7822. In 1952 trials took place using No. 7818 *Granville Manor* to investigate the steaming problems which revealed an output of only 10,000 lbs of steam per hour, less than half of the amount a 'Hall' could produce. The chimney and blastpipe diameter were reduced and the space between the firebars slightly increased. The result was a better fed combustion chamber and a sharper exhaust, and the steam production more than doubled to over 20,000 lbs per hour, completely transforming the engines. No less than nine of the thirty engines in the 'Manor' class have been preserved, all except one coming out of Woodham's scrapyard at Barry Docks. Note below the Down starter is the 'shunt ahead' signal arm with the large letter 'S'; this authorised a driver to enter the single line as far as was necessary to clear the points to cross over on to the Up line.

W.J.V. Anderson/Rail Archive Stephenson

CHAPTER 3 - BALA JUNCTION TO BARMOUTH JUNCTION (MORFA MAWDDACH)   29

Although the town's name officially changed to Dolgellau in 1958 the station did not follow suit until September 1960. Lined green liveried BR Standard Class '3' 2-6-2T No. 82033 stands in the Down platform on a westbound local in August 1963. The former Cambrian Railways station building situated on this platform had an ornate carved end screen to the canopy, a steeply pitched roof and three chimneys. No. 82033 was transferred from Bristol Barrow Road to Machynlleth at the end of 1960 and worked on the Cambrian until mid-1964.

BR Standard Class '4' 4-6-0 No. 75029 at Dolgellau with an eastbound train on 3rd October 1964. Visible in this view on the left are the former Cambrian Railways' buildings situated on the Down platform; the GWR building opposite, mostly hidden by the train, had a much shallower roof and twin pavilions with gable ends facing the platform. When the GWR modernised the station in the early 1920s they replaced the signalling and the signal box and built a new passenger footbridge.

Penmaenpool

BR Standard Class '2' 2-6-0 No. 78006 pilots GWR '43XX' 2-6-0 No. 6357 as they arrive at Penmaenpool on a Penychain to Birmingham summer special in August 1958. No. 78006 was the first of the class repainted in lined green livery by Swindon Works, in March 1957; it was at Machynlleth from September 1953 until September 1962. No. 6357 had been transferred to Tyseley from Shrewsbury in May 1958. The small, two-road shed in the distance was built by the Cambrian Railways to house the engines which worked the 'shuttle' service between Dolgelley and Barmouth. The shed became a sub-shed to Croes Newydd in Wrexham, although locomotives would visit Machynlleth for minor servicing. The Mawddach river is on the right with the two men in the rowing boat paying no attention to the passing train.

On a Barmouth-Dolgellau 'shuttle', Ivatt 2-6-0 No. 46521 at Penmaenpool, probably in 1964 since it has a 6F Machynlleth shed plate which did not come into effect until September 1963. After withdrawal from Machynlleth in October 1966 No. 46521 went to Woodham's scrapyard at Barry from where it was purchased for preservation in 1971 by a Severn Valley Railway member. It was the first ex-Barry restoration on that railway and entered service in July 1974, working until 1977 when it was withdrawn for major boiler repairs. Following completion of the overhaul, it worked until 1985 and returned to service again from 1991 until 2000. It was moved to the Great Central Railway for overhaul in November 2001, which involved extensive repairs to the boiler and firebox, and did not steam again until the end of 2011. It has worked on several preserved lines since then and is currently operational.

These two pictures of Croes Newydd's double-chimneyed BR Standard Class '4' 4-6-0 No. 75006 at Penmaenpool in 1964 show how close the railway was to the edge of the Mawddach Estuary.

Above: The signalman waits on the Up platform to exchange the single line tokens as No. 75006 arrives from Barmouth. On the right below the running-in board, can be glimpsed the wooden toll-bridge over to the small village of Bontddu, whose name was somewhat optimistically included on the boards in the early years of the line. The bridge was given Grade II listed status in 1990 and today costs vehicles 60p to cross. The Down platform, where this picture was taken from, was added when the Great Western Railway modernised the station after the 1923 Grouping and was offset from the original Up platform where the signalman is standing. The signal box had been part of the GWR's exhibit at the 1925 Wembley Exhibition, after which it was dismantled, stored at Reading signal works, and erected nine years later at Penmaenpool. It has a commanding view of the Mawddach Estuary and is still in use today as an observation centre by the Royal Society for the Protection of Birds.

Below: No. 75006 has returned with a train back to Barmouth and the crew are now talking to the same signalman who is on the Down platform. Both platforms were boarded with timber and each had a wooden waiting shelter. The line behind the Down platform served a small goods yard and in this picture are three open wagons which were kept there until needed at the nearby engine shed.

Morfa Mawddach (Barmouth Junction)

The station was opened in 1872 and had two pairs of through platforms and a bay. The line which came up from Machynlleth and Towyn formed a triangular junction with the coastal line to Barmouth and Pwllheli to the west and the Dolgelley line to the east; the southern side of the triangle did not have a platform and was used either to turn locomotives or as freight sidings.

On 13th June 1960 the station was renamed from Barmouth Junction, ostensibly to avoid confusion for passengers who mistook it for Barmouth across the estuary. All that remains today is a basic station on the coastal line from Machynlleth to Barmouth, the Dolgelley line having been closed in January 1965.

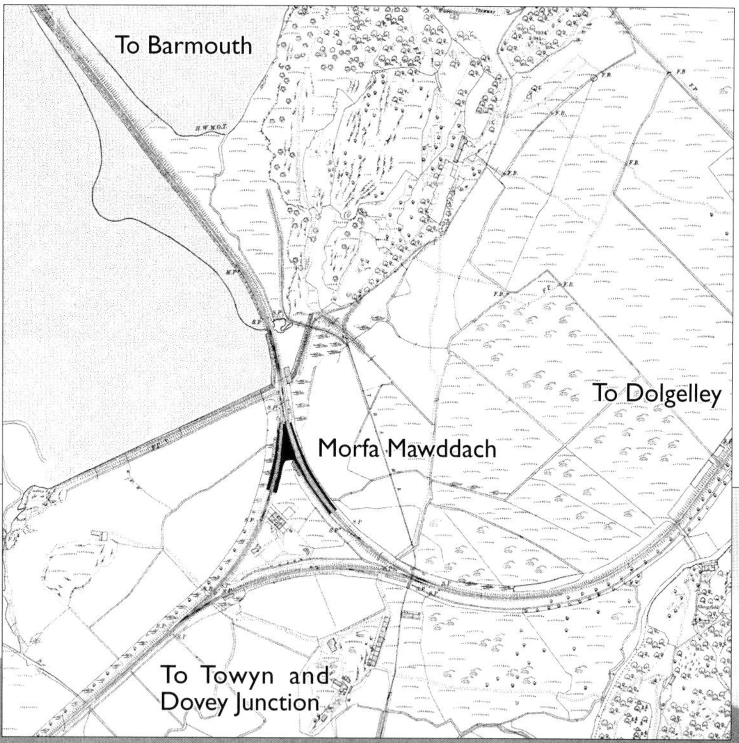

No. 7817 *Garsington Manor* arriving from Dolgelley is about to pass one of the large running-in boards at Morfa Mawddach. Apart from a few weeks in late 1958 at Shrewsbury, No. 7817 was at Croes Newydd from new in 1939 until February 1961 when it went to Stourbridge Junction. It was the first of class to work between Ruabon and Barmouth when it undertook clearance tests in 1940. There was another large board on the Down Coast platform advising passengers 'TO CHANGE FOR DOLGELLEY, BALA, CORWEN, LLANGOLLEN, RUABON AND CHESTER'.

No. 7818 *Granville Manor* enters Morfa Mawddach with the 1.55pm Barmouth-Machynlleth train on 24th August 1963. It moved to Machynlleth in January 1960 from Newton Abbot and stayed until withdrawn in January 1965. On the left is one of the small wooden huts provided to give passengers some shelter from the elements at this exposed location; there was another similar one on the Up Dolgellau platform.

Robert Darlaston

Ivatt Class '2' 2-6-0 No. 46446 on the Barmouth-Dolgellau 'shuttle' in the 1960s. It was built at Crewe in March 1950 and based on the London Midland Region in the Midlands at Coventry, Nuneaton and then Rugby until May 1963 when it moved to the Cambrian at Machynlleth; it saw out its days there until withdrawal at the end of 1966.

Ivatt 2-6-0 No. 46511 takes the District Engineer's Inspection saloon coach No. W80972W from Morfa Mawddach towards Barmouth on 22nd May 1962. The Engineers used the saloon which was still resplendent in 'chocolate and cream' to travel from their headquarters at Oswestry when inspecting their District. The smokebox of No. 46511 is adorned with a home-made headboard containing the three Prince of Wales' feathers with the words 'Engineer's Inspection' below.

Ivatt 2-6-0 No. 46512 departs from Morfa Mawddach with the 1.41pm Dolgelley-Barmouth local on 24th August 1963. It was built at Swindon in December 1952 and was allocated to Oswestry from then until January 1965 when the shed was closed, and it was transferred to Shrewsbury. The licensed station refreshment rooms in the main station building in the fork of the Dolgellau and Machynlleth platforms were also used as a local pub, complete with dartboard and mat.

Robert Darlaston

At the north west end of the Morfa Mawddach triangle double-chimneyed BR Standard Class '4MT' No. 75006 with a train for Barmouth in 1963. To the left of the rear coach is one of the three green and cream-painted camping coaches that were stabled there for many years. The line from Dolgellau is on the left and to the right, the line to Towyn and Machynlleth.

CHAPTER 3 - BALA JUNCTION TO BARMOUTH JUNCTION (MORFA MAWDDACH)

Croes Newydd's BR Standard Class '4' 4-6-0 No. 75023 waits at the signals in the Barmouth platform with a train from Dolgelley on 3rd October 1964. Note the Scottish Region allocated ex-LM&SR Stanier coach No. SC 2436 M leading. The station originally had three signal boxes but the Great Western replaced them in 1931 by one new box at the Barmouth end of the triangle. This controlled all train movements, with special instructions in force when locomotives used the triangle for turning. It was named Barmouth Junction Signal Box and had a thirty-eight lever frame; the signalman also controlled the single line token equipment to Barmouth South, Llwyngwril and Penmaenpool.

On the same day, No. 75023 leaves a smokescreen across Barmouth Bay as it approaches Morfa Mawddach on its return from Barmouth. In the background is Garn Gorllwyn at 870ft, the ground eventually rising to 1,689ft at Bwlch y Rhiwgyr.

BR Standard Class '3' 2-6-2T No. 82003 waiting with a train for Barmouth and Pwllheli, with the station's main platform on the left in this view. No. 82003 was one of the first of the class to be painted in lined green livery during overhaul at Swindon Works, emerging from there in May 1957. The Standard 2-6-2Ts had replaced the GWR '45XX' and '4575' 2-6-2Ts on the Cambrian in 1960/1. Their principal duties were on local trains between Machynlleth and Pwllheli working three-day cyclical rosters – with an overall speed limit of 55mph, nineteen stations and twelve halts this was the type of work they had been built for.

Another picture of No. 82003 which havivng left Morfa Mawddach is now skirting the bay towards Barmouth, probably on a Dovey Junction-Pwllheli train in 1963. It had been transferred from Carmarthen to Machynlleth in June 1962 and ended its days at Patricroft, from March 1965 until December 1966.

Running bunker-first, BR Standard Class '3' 2-6-2T No. 82009 has come up from the coastal line from Towyn in 1963. It had been transferred from Bristol St. Philip's Marsh to Machynlleth in February 1961 and was there until its transfer to Patricroft in 1965. It was one of five of the class working from the sub-shed at Pwllheli at this date. On the left of the young enthusiast is the third side of the triangle at Morfa Mawddach which did not have any platform faces and was mainly used for turning tender locomotives in the busy holiday season since Barmouth had only a short 45ft turntable, and this was removed in the 1950s. On busy summer Saturdays there was a constant stream of engines, sometimes coupled together, arriving from Barmouth to turn.

Times changed quickly on the Cambrian after January 1965 and not only regarding the motive power; the redundant arms have been removed from the bracket signal following the closure of the Dolgelley line. BR Sulzer Type '2' No. D5039 was on a freight heading from Aberystwyth to Barmouth at Morfa Mawddach in 1968. The Class '24' diesel-electric went from new at Derby Works to Ipswich in September 1959 and remained on the Eastern Region until August 1967 when it was transferred to the LMR Stoke Division, staying in the area until withdrawn in 1976 as TOPS No. 24039.

4 – Morfa Mawddach (Barmouth Junction) to Pwllheli

The Aberystwith & Welsh Coast Railway was authorised in 1861 to build a line from Machynlleth to Aberystwyth and from Dovey Junction to Barmouth and Portmadoc, extended in 1862 to Pwllheli. The section from Barmouth Junction to Pwllheli opened in October 1867, two years after the company became part of the Cambrian Railways.

Closure of the line from Dovey Junction via Barmouth to Pwllheli was proposed in 1967, but fortunately it survived and is now marketed as the 'Cambrian Coast Railway'.

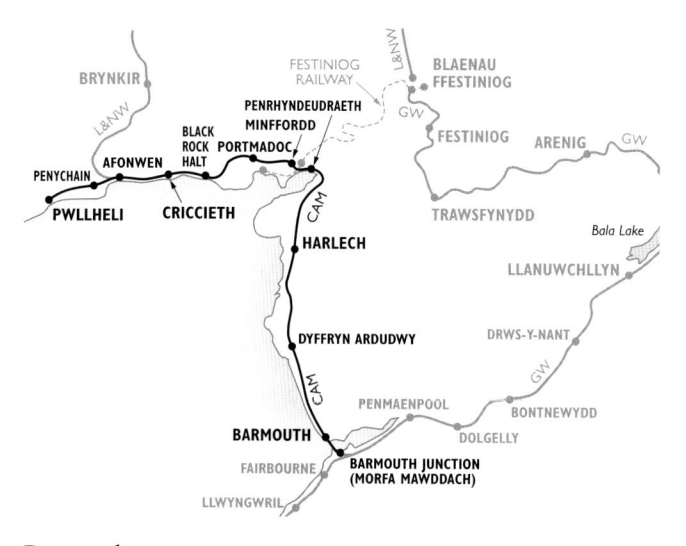

Barmouth

Situated on a very narrow strip of land between the sea and the mountains, Barmouth developed after the arrival of the railway into a popular resort, bringing lots of summer traffic to the town. It was served from the north by the line from Portmadoc, from the east via Dolgelley and the south from Machynlleth, the latter two meeting at Barmouth Junction before crossing over the Mawddach Estuary on the now iconic Barmouth viaduct.

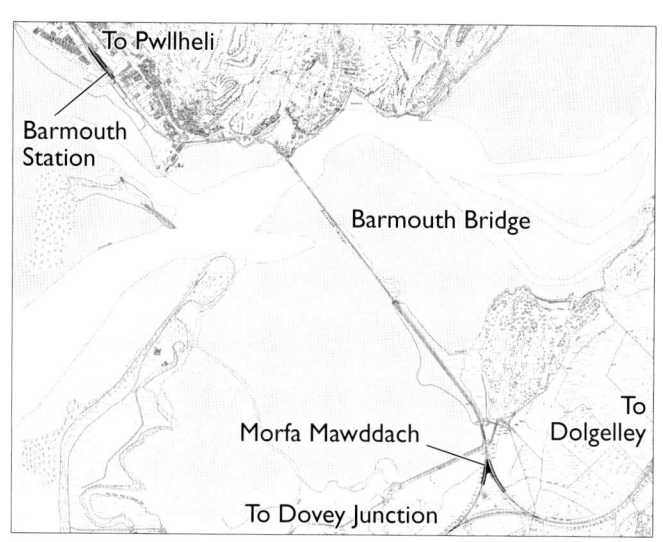

'Barmouth Bridge'

The 800 yards long viaduct across the Mawddach Estuary, known locally as 'Barmouth Bridge', had three sections, the longest of which was a series of 113 spans, each around eighteen feet long, made up of wooden trestles built on over 500 timber piles. Next, over a 50ft channel in the deepest part of the estuary, was an 'overdraw' iron bridge comprising one opening and seven fixed spans. It was replaced in 1900 by four steel spans, one of which was a swing span revolving on a centre pier, giving two clear openings below; the final pair of fixed spans at the Barmouth end were replaced by shallow lattice girders. The piers carrying the girders were eight feet diameter columns, sunk through the sand onto solid rock. A toll footpath was included alongside the track which became very popular not only with visitors, but also with local people who used the shelters provided along the length. In addition to pedestrians, the path was used by people on bicycles, tandems and even motorcycles.

With the 2,927ft high Cader Idris in the background. Churchward '43XX' 2-6-0 No. 5393 has just crossed Barmouth Bridge with an eight-coach express and approaches the town on 14th May 1951. It was built in 1920 and renumbered to 8393 in 1928 when fitted with a heavy casting behind the front buffer beam to reduce wear on the flanges of the leading coupled wheels. It reverted to No. 5393 in September 1948, the last of over sixty of the class which had been similarly modified to be reinstated to its previous condition; it has still not been fitted with a smokebox number plate.

The engine is passing over the former slipway used by the lifeboat before the latter found a new home on the promenade. The rear of the train is on the moveable steel section which was built on 8ft diameter piers sunk to a depth of about 90ft below the high-water level. In 1980 examiners found half of the wooden part had been attacked by the *Teredo Navalis* naval shipworm threatening closure of the Cambrian Coast Line, but after expensive repair work the bridge was fully re-opened six years later.

John Wilson/Rail Archive Stephenson

CHAPTER 4 - MORFA MAWDDACH (BARMOUTH JUNCTION) TO PWLLHELI

GWR '4575' class 2-6-2T No. 4599 has just crossed the viaduct and approaches the town with a local train from Machynlleth on 25th June 1955. It was allocated to Machynlleth from October 1953, its third time there, until withdrawn in March 1959. The swing bridge featured in the 1941 film 'The Ghost Train' in which, by using a combination of scale models and trick photography, a train loaded with smuggled ammunition appeared to plunge from the 'opened' bridge into the waters below. The line left the viaduct on a sharp curve, hence the check rail, before passing through a short tunnel.
T.G. Hepburn/Rail Archive Stephenson

A BR Standard Class '2' 2-6-0 heads towards Barmouth Junction in July 1957 with a fascinating train consisting of an ex-Southern Railway brake van, a rake of three GWR Collett coaches, a GWR four-wheeled former five-compartment Diag. S9 coach (in departmental use) and at the rear a LM&SR Diagram 1661 unfitted cattle wagon. Over 2,000 of the latter were built between 1923 and 1926 and they were in use until the early 1960s.

With Cader Idris, the second highest mountain in Wales in the background, a Barmouth-bound passenger train headed by a '90XX' 4-4-0 crosses the half-mile long Barmouth Bridge stretching away across the Mawddach estuary. Three men in a rowing boat enjoy a trip in the tranquil waters.

Ivatt class '2' 2-6-0 No 46521 on the swing bridge section of the viaduct leaves Barmouth behind with a pick-up goods for Machynlleth on 25th July 1963. To open the swing bridge, a key had to be obtained from an instrument in the signal box at Barmouth to unlock ground frames on the moveable section and which at the same time prevented trains from crossing onto the bridge. Then two lengths of rail at each end were removed to allow the swing section to be turned; telephone and other cables also had to be temporarily disconnected. The drive was transmitted through rods and gears from cranked handles powered by the efforts of around half a dozen PW men at the centre pivot point. Opening took between half and three-quarters of an hour, depending on weather conditions and especially the strength of the wind. The bridge was difficult to close when the steel expanded in the height summer and on some occasions this could not be done until it had cooled down sufficiently overnight. This meant that it was only opened infrequently, sometimes only once a year, to check it was in working order and usually on a Sunday to prevent disruption to summer traffic; it was last opened over twenty years ago. On the right is the pedestrian walkway for which users had to pay a small toll, and beyond is the small cottage occupied by the toll keeper.

Brian Stephenson

Left: The summit of Craig y Llyn is hidden in the clouds as No. 7818 *Granville Manor* runs light, tender-first, across the viaduct to turn on the triangle at Morfa Mawddach before working the 1.55pm Barmouth to Machynlleth on 24th August 1963. No. 7818 moved to Machynlleth in January 1960 from Newton Abbot and was withdrawn from there in January 1965. A number of huts were provided along the length of the half-mile long, 8ft 3in. wide walkway to give shelter to pedestrians. *Robert Darlaston*

A handful of people are on the beach and exploring the rock pools as Machynlleth's Ivatt Class '2' 2-6-0 No. 46521 comes off the viaduct with the 5.5pm SX from Dolgellau on 7th August 1964.

Barmouth approaches

'2251' 0-6-0 No. 2286 has just passed over Cumberland Place level crossing after leaving the station with a Barmouth to Dovey Junction stopper in 1957. It is threading its way between the houses on the promontory before crossing 'Old Chapel Viaduct' and entering the short tunnel ahead of the 'Bridge'. It was at Machynlleth from July 1955 until October 1962 when it was transferred to Hereford.

'90XX' 4-4-0 No. 9015 emerges from the rock tunnel as it approaches Barmouth station with a train from Machynlleth on 8th September 1956. The tunnel was only seventy yards long and was very unusual because above it was a cutting through which a road passed. Allocated the name *Earl of Clancarty*, No. 9015 entered service at Didcot as plain No. 3215 in October 1937 and worked on the Didcot, Newbury and Southampton line along with No. 3206. It was renumbered as 9015 at Didcot shed in 1946 and moved to Machynlleth from Oxford in July 1956. No. 9015 has tapered buffers, no top feed and non-standard cab windows inherited from its predecessor 'Duke' No. 3262; it was withdrawn in June 1960.

C.R.L. Coles/Rail Archive Stephenson

This '4575' 2-6-2T has passed through the tunnel and is on the 'Old Chapel Viaduct' heading towards Barmouth station. The six-span viaduct was 78 yards long and the original wooden structure had been rebuilt in concrete in 1952. It is low tide as is evident from the boats moored on the mud in the foreground.

BR Standard Class '2' 2-6-0 No. 78000 is about to pass through the tunnel and over the bridge in around 1957. The Standard 2-6-0s were dimensionally almost identical with the Swindon-built Ivatt engines, although they naturally incorporated BR standard fittings together with a redesigned cab with sloping upper side sheets and sloping front footplate ahead of the cylinders. They had the BR No. 8 boiler which was very similar to the LMS No. 7 boiler used on the Ivatt 2-6-0s and 2-6-2Ts, but with a revised water delivery from a side clack valve arrangement rather than top feed, and the regulator was a vertical grid type operated by an external rod at the side of the firebox. The BR design weighed 2 tons 3 cwt more and had the same tractive effort as the later Ivatt engines. The first batch of ten was built at Darlington between December 1952 and April 1953, at the same time as Swindon was completing the last of the Ivatt 2-6-0s. Nos. 78000-9 initially went to Oswestry for use on the mid-Wales lines, but Nos. 78000-5 were soon transferred to Machynlleth, in April/May 1953. No. 78000 remained there until May 1963 when it was transferred to Nottingham. This picture shows how the buildings in Barmouth were built into the adjoining hillside; the waters of Cardigan Bay are just visible in the gap between the buildings in the background.

CHAPTER 4 - MORFA MAWDDACH (BARMOUTH JUNCTION) TO PWLLHELI

BR Standard Class '3' 2-6-2T No.82033 leaves Barmouth with the 10.25am Pwllheli to Dovey Junction train on 25th July 1963. It was transferred from Bristol Barrow Road to Machynlleth at the end of 1960 and worked on the Cambrian until mid-1964. No.82033 was one of several of the 2-6-2Ts sub-shedded at Portmadoc until the depot closed in August 1963, after which the class operated from Pwllheli. On the left of the picture overlooking the harbour is The Quay road which passed beneath the railway under a low bridge at the end of Old Chapel Viaduct. *Brian Stephenson*

Barmouth station

Barmouth station in Cambrian Railways days was small with station buildings which struggled to cope with passengers when a London express arrived. Immediately after the 1923 Grouping, the Great Western extended the platforms to accommodate longer trains and raised them to its standard height. Special arrangements allowed two trains to use each platform when necessary. At the south end a new bay platform was built on the Up side which had separate access from the rest of the station because it was on the other side of the road which crossed the line on the level at the south end of the original platforms. Its main use was for the Dolgelley shuttle but was also used for excursion traffic. The signalling was also upgraded at both the South and North signal boxes.

'90XX' 4-4-0 No. 9005 and a Collett '2251' 0-6-0 arrive at Barmouth from the south in July 1956 shortly after the 'Dukedog' was transferred from Machynlleth to Oswestry following a recent overhaul at Swindon Works. No. 9005 was built in September 1936 as No. 3205 using the frames from 'Bulldog' No. 3413 and the cab and other parts from 'Duke' No. 3255. It was named *Earl of Devon* until 1937 and was renumbered as 9005 in July 1946. Platform 4 on the left was the new platform added in the early 1920s which had its own separate ticket office that was opened as and when required. The funfair on the right with swing-boats and dodgems does not look very busy even though this was the start of the summer holiday season. Note the 5mph speed restriction sign and the loading gauge above the coach in the bay platform. The end of the bay was occasionally used as a loading ramp and the gauge was positioned there to ensure that loaded wagons did not foul bridges and structures along the line, especially the route to Aberdovey which was notoriously 'tight'.

CHAPTER 4 - MORFA MAWDDACH (BARMOUTH JUNCTION) TO PWLLHELI

Resplendent in BR lined black mixed traffic livery, Collett '14XX' 0-4-2T No. 1465 with the auto train for Dolgelley on 14th May 1951. Formerly No. 4865 until October 1946, it was allocated to Machynlleth until late 1956 when it spent a few weeks at Slough before returning to Wales at Croes Newydd. At this date it was deputising for the regular engine, No. 1434 based at the Penmaenpool sub-shed, which was unavailable. No. 1465 had an unfortunate accident in 1954 while working the auto train at Arthog when the spokes fractured in its left-hand trailing wheel; Crosville buses provided a temporary 'rail-replacement' service. The journey time for the 'shuttle' between Barmouth and Dolgelley was twenty-seven minutes, which was unchanged since the 1930s.

John P. Wilson/Rail Archive Stephenson

'90XX' 4-4-0 No. 9014 from Machynlleth shed leaves Barmouth with a train for Pwllheli on 14th May 1951. It was rebuilt from 'Duke' No. 3252 *Duke of Cornwall* and 'Bulldog' No. 3434 *Joseph Shaw* and entered traffic in August 1937 unnamed. It was one of only two of the class to receive fully lined out BR black livery, applied in 1949. The class was fitted with ATC equipment and the shoe is visible below the bufferbeam. No. 9014 was one of the last two to be withdrawn, in October 1960. On the right the bay platform contains four coaches and a '45XX' 2-6-2T is passing over the turntable, perhaps to couple on to them. To the left of No. 9014 is the large goods shed outside which stands a former L&SWR outside framed van and an ancient GWR four-plank open with 'ED' painted on its side indicating it was in Engineering Department service.

John P. Wilson/Rail Archive Stephenson

CHAPTER 4 - MORFA MAWDDACH (BARMOUTH JUNCTION) TO PWLLHELI

'45XX' 2-6-2T No. 4549 after arrival at Barmouth with a train from Pwllheli on 14th May 1951. It was at Machynlleth from 1938 until 1960, moving to the south west at Laira and ending its days in Cornwall at Penzance from where it was withdrawn in December 1961. The composition of the train is quite eclectic – leading is a GWR D115 right-handed Brake Third with inset guards door built in 1932, followed by a GWR C30 Bars 1 Toplight of 1910, then what appears to be a LM&SR Stanier all Third of the mid-1930s, and the final vehicle with its small windows is probably a GWR D103 bow-ended Brake Third of 1929.
John P. Wilson/Rail Archive Stephenson

On the same day another '45XX', Machynlleth's No. 4555, has passed the Barmouth North signal box as it sets off for Pwllheli. At this date Machynlleth had four of its engines shedded nightly at Pwllheli and No. 4555 would have been one of those. It left the Cambrian in October 1957 for Westbury and ended its days at Laira. After withdrawal at the end of 1963 it was purchased for preservation by Patrick Whitehouse and Pat Garland. No. 4555 worked on the Dart Valley Railway for several years and is currently on the Dartmouth Steam Railway. It is not operational and is near the end of a full overhaul after which it is due to go to the East Somerset Railway for two years.
John P. Wilson/Rail Archive Stephenson

BR Standard Class '2' 2-6-0 No. 78003 passes Barmouth South signal box with a northbound train in the mid-1950s. The first ten of the class went initially to Oswestry but Nos.78000-7 were there for only a short time and moved to Machynlleth; No. 78003 was transferred in April 1953. They worked between Shrewsbury, Oswestry and the Cambrian Coast including the Aberystwyth and Pwllheli portions of the 'Cambrian Coast Express' in summer 1954, taking it through to Shrewsbury. However, they struggled to cope when the train loaded to more than seven coaches and 'Manor' 4-6-0s and '43XX' 2-6-0s took over from the start of the winter timetable. They did continue to work the Aberystwyth-Shrewsbury stopping trains. A '58XX' 0-4-2T, either No. 5803 or 5809 which were both allocated to Machynlleth at this date, will run round the coaches for the Dolgelley 'shuttle' in Platform 4. Behind the signal box is the Crosville bus office and the single-decker bus with the 'Corona' advertisement on the side is a Bristol LWL with bodywork by ECW.

It is 4.12pm according to the church clock in the background as BR Standard Class '2' 2-6-0 No. 78006 waits in the excursion platform with two corridor coaches forming the Dolgelley 'shuttle'. One of the Machynlleth 2-6-0s was regularly sub-shedded at Penmaenpool to work this service in the late 1950s. The first ten Standard 2-6-0s, Nos.78000-9, were delivered to Oswestry for use on the mid-Wales lines but within a few months the first six were transferred to Machynlleth in April/May 1953 and worked between Shrewsbury, Oswestry and the Cambrian Coast, and also on Talerddig banking duties; No. 78006 followed six months later. This picture dates from around 1958/9 with No. 78006 in the lined green livery which it received in March 1957; it stayed at Machynlleth until October 1962. The turreted building in the centre background was an English Congregational Chapel built at the end of the nineteenth century. In the late 1950s it was converted into a theatre for the community, opening in October 1959, and continues in use today as 'The Dragon Theatre and Barmouth Community Centre'.

Barmouth had to build upwards because of the limited space between Garn Gorllwyn on the right and the Cardigan Bay shoreline. The residents of these flats in the five-storey building overlooking the station would have had a grandstand view of the railway operations as well as the sea beyond. On the ground floor were several cafes, grill rooms and a fish and chip restaurant. In front, '2251' class 0-6-0 No. 2255 in passenger lined green livery stands at Platform 4 with a train for Ruabon in August 1959. It was at Machynlleth from July 1955 until withdrawn in May 1962 and was one of the first batch of Collett's modernised version of the 'Dean Goods', entering service in March 1930. *J.F. Davies/Rail Archive Stephenson*

There are lots of holidaymakers around the station as '74XX' 0-6-0PT No. 7442 waits to leave Barmouth with the 'shuttle' to Dolgellau in September 1961. Machynlleth provided the motive power for these local trains and No. 7442 was there from September 1961 until February 1962, going to Croes Newydd for a few weeks in early 1962 and returning there until early 1963. In the background a BR Standard Class '3' 2-6-2T on a freight is held at the level crossing gates which were in the middle of the station layout. Barmouth South signal box is on the left and the station building is visible above the rear coach. The footbridge was divided in two lengthwise, one side for railway passengers and the other for pedestrians to access the beach area when the level-crossing gates were closed.
Stephen Summerson/Rail Archive Stephenson

Churchward '43XX' 2-6-0 No. 5330 backs into Barmouth station after turning on the triangle at Morfa Mawddach and awaits its next turn on a busy Summer Saturday, 30th June 1962. It had recently been transferred to Croes Newydd from Newport Ebbw Junction; it stayed there until October 1963. Further back at the end of the excursion platform is another 2-6-0, No. 7341 which was the last '43XX' when built in April 1932, and a BR 2-6-2T; No. 5330 was built in September 1917.

One of the class built during the Second World War, this picture of '2251' 0-6-0 No. 2222 was taken in the second half of 1960 after it moved from Shrewsbury to Croes Newydd and before it left there in November for Machynlleth. It looks like No. 2222 is coupled to one of the smaller capacity narrow tenders. As there is no brake van at the rear No. 2222 must be shunting and needs to get out of the way soon because there are lots of customers waiting for the next passenger service.

Green-liveried BR Standard Class '4' 4-6-0 No. 75004 pulls in with a southbound train in 1963. It has an 89C shed plate and had been transferred to Machynlleth from Bath Green Park in the four weeks ended 3rd November 1962 and was fitted with a double chimney at Swindon in October 1962.

Passengers on Platform 2 waiting for their train to Pwllheli watch a return holiday express from Pwllheli to Birmingham Snow Hill double-headed by BR Standard Class '2' 2-6-0 No. 78007 and BR Standard Class '3' 2-6-2T No. 82033 on 30th June 1962. Both Machynlleth allocated engines had received green livery at Swindon Works, No. 78007 was unlined whereas No. 82033 had GWR-style orange/black/orange lining.

CHAPTER 4 - MORFA MAWDDACH (BARMOUTH JUNCTION) TO PWLLHELI

The sun is shining as BR Standard Class '3' 2-6-2T No. 82034 awaits the 'Right-away' from Platform 2 on a local train to Portmadoc and Pwllheli. It has a 6F shedplate dating the picture between September 1963 and April 1965 when it moved from Machynlleth to Patricroft and therefore probably was taken in summer 1964.

The long platforms extended by the GWR in the 1920s show up well in this picture of No. 7823 *Hook Norton Manor* at the north end of the station after arriving with an excursion from the Midlands. It was allocated to Truro until April 1959 when it was transferred to Machynlleth but by this date was at Tyseley to where it moved in November 1962 and was withdrawn from there in July 1964.

There is lots of activity on Platform 2 as BR Standard Class '4' 4-6-0 No. 75021 blows off from its safety valves. It was at Croes Newydd from March 1964 until April 1967 apart from four months at Shrewsbury in early 1966 and this picture was probably taken in 1966. Underneath the grime No. 75021 was still in the green livery it had since February 1959 and it had kept its original single chimney unlike a number of other Western Region classmates. Note on the right the BR coach brake cylinder on the platform – a heavy item to move in a passenger brake van!

CHAPTER 4 - MORFA MAWDDACH (BARMOUTH JUNCTION) TO PWLLHELI

Diesels

At the end of 1966 the majority of steam workings ceased on the Shrewsbury-Aberystwyth line, with the exception of the Up and Down 'Cambrian Coast Express' which lasted until March 1967. In January 1967 Class '24' diesels from Shrewsbury, now part of the D05 Stoke Division, were diagrammed for Cambrian line working and would operate these services for the next seven years. The transfer to the D05 Division of eleven Class '24's in March 1967 and thirteen more in April allowed driver training to commence from Croes Newydd shed.

Class '24' No. D5077, paired with No. D5055, awaits departure from Barmouth with a return excursion, probably in late 1968 or early 1969. It has three-piece miniature snowploughs but these were soon taken off following several recorded incidents of them damaging the check rails on Barmouth bridge. No. D5077 was built at Crewe in February 1960 and went to the Eastern Region at March before moving to Willesden in July. After completion of the London Midland Region electrification to London it was transferred in December 1966 to the Stoke Division. No. D5055 also went to March when new in December 1959 but moved around more than its classmate, spending time in Scotland and the North West before arriving at the Stoke Division in September 1968. Renumbered as 24077 and 24055 under TOPS in 1974, they were withdrawn in July 1976 and October 1975 respectively.

Another Class '24' pairing waits behind the level crossing gates at Barmouth in 1972, No. 5054 in corporate blue livery and No. 5057 still in green but with full yellow ends. Both were delivered from Crewe Works to the Eastern Region at March in December 1959 and were transferred to Finsbury Park in January 1961. After that, their paths diverged, No. 5054 going to Eastfield in 1966 while No. 5057 moved to the LMR London Division. They were re-united in the Stoke Division, with 5057 arriving first in April 1967 and 5054 following in September 1968. No. 5057 was withdrawn in January 1978 as TOPS No. 24057, but No. 5054 is still with us today. It went into Departmental service as carriage heating unit No. ADB968008 following withdrawal in July 1976 and was subsequently purchased for preservation by the East Lancashire Railway.

Dyffryn Ardudwy

'90XX' 4-4-0 No. 9013 with the Pwllheli portion of the 'Cambrian Coast Express' approaching Dyffryn Ardudwy, the station midway between Barmouth and Harlech. No. 9013 was always on the Cambrian, from July 1937 until December 1958 when it was condemned at Machynlleth; it had been allocated the name *Earl of Powis* but was the first 'Dukedog' to enter traffic unnamed. The 'Cambrian Coast Express' originated from a Saturdays Only train in the 1920 summer timetable from Paddington with through portions for Aberystwyth and Pwllheli. This service was given the name in 1927 and it continued until the Second World War when it was suspended. It was reintroduced in 1947 without its name, which was not restored until June 1954. The Down train divided at Machynlleth into portions for Aberystwyth and Pwllheli. During 1957 it usually loaded to ten coaches – six for Aberystwyth and four for Pwllheli as in this picture, and by 1959 it was running every weekday.

Machynlleth's BR Standard Class '2' 2-6-0 No. 78003 departs from Dyffryn Ardudwy with a Pwllheli to Birmingham service via Ruabon in the mid-1950s. The cast iron SW sign means 'Sound Whistle' and is of standard GWR pattern.

Harlech

During the 1950s there were several 'Land Cruise' trains which took summer holidaymakers on circular tours around North Wales. The London Midland Region trains started from Rhyl and Llandudno and the Western Region one from Pwllheli. They went under various names including the 'North Wales Land Cruise', the 'Cambrian Radio Land Cruise' and the 'North Wales Radio Land Cruise' as illustrated by a BR Standard Class '4' 4-6-0 at Harlech in 1957. The Western Region service started in 1954 and the promotional leaflet for the train advertised it as *'Specially equipped for actual radio reception and descriptive commentary on features of interest en route'*. It started at Pwllheli and ran via Barmouth, Corwen, Rhyl and Bangor and back to Barmouth from July until early September. The cruises ended in summer 1961 following the closure of the Corwen to Denbigh and the Afon Wen to Bangor lines. The Ivatt Class '2' 2-6-0s and '2251' Class 0-6-0s worked the trains until 1956, but their increasing popularity required six or even seven coaches and more powerful engines were needed. In 1957 BR Standard Class '4' 4-6-0s took over following the raising of the route restriction from 'Yellow' to 'Blue' between Dovey Junction and Barmouth and along the coast, because the outside-cylinder '43XX' and 'Manor' classes were too wide to run over some of the ex-L&NWR lines involved in the itinerary.

Probably on the same day as the above photograph with low cloud and not a soul in sight, '4575' 2-6-2T No. 5507 has just travelled along the four mile long straight section of line from the north at Talsarnau across Morfa Harlech with a freight comprised solely of open wagons, some possibly carrying slate, although the length of the train suggests another traffic. The 1927-built 'Prairie' was allocated to Machynlleth in April 1947 and was there until withdrawn in August 1958. On the right are the tree-covered lower slopes of 1,211ft Moel Goedog and in the distance mostly hidden by the clouds, is the 2,527ft high Moelwyn Mawr which towers above the Vale of Ffestiniog. The elderly ex-GWR coach on the right could well be one of two grounded bodies mounted on blocks and used at this time as goods offices and stores, serving the freight loop running behind the southbound platform.

'4575' 2-6-2T No. 5570 was at Machynlleth from 1936 until February 1960 when it moved to Penzance. Its fireman on the northbound local is about to give the single line token to the signalman leaning out of Harlech Signal Box, by far the preferred procedure rather than using the apparatus provided. The crossing in the foreground was known as Morfa Level Crossing, on a lane to a school and a few cottages on Morfa Harlech. It was controlled by the 27-lever cabin and usually the gates were closed to road traffic. Behind the train is Morfa Crossing on the B4573 from Harlech, which ran parallel to the railway across the flatlands; the gates were normally open for road vehicles and operated by the crossing keeper.

'90XX' 4-4-0 No. 9014 leaving Harlech with the four-coach Pwllheli portion of the 'Cambrian Coast Express' which it had taken over at Machynlleth, where the train divided, with six coaches going forward to Aberystwyth behind the 'Manor' which had brought them from Shrewsbury. This picture was probably taken in 1956, the final year the '90XX' 4-4-0s regularly worked the train. No. 9014 was allocated the name *Earl Waldegrave* but it was always unnamed and instead the name went to 'Castle' No. 5057. No. 9014 was at Machynlleth until July 1957 moving to Croes Newydd from where it was withdrawn in October 1960.

BR Standard Class '2' 2-6-0 No. 78007 with a long Class '8' freight which, unusually for this line, appears not to include any gunpowder vans. The 2-6-0 went new to Oswestry in March 1953 and moved on to Machynlleth six months later; it left the Cambrian in September 1962 going to Gloucester Barnwood.

With the Castle in the background, BR Standard Class '3' 2-6-2T No. 82020 waits at Harlech on a Pwllheli train in the early 1960s. The class was built to work on routes where there was a maximum axle loading of 16 tons, well below the 20 tons of the Standard Class '4' 2-6-4Ts, and which needed a more powerful engine than the Class '2' 2-6-2T based on the LM&SR Ivatt design. They had a modified Swindon No. 4 boiler as used on the GWR '51XX' and '81XX' 2-6-2Ts and the '56XX' 0-6-2Ts. Nos.82031 and 82020 arrived on the Cambrian at Machynlleth in early 1960 and by the end of 1961 the shed had nine of the class on its books. Two years later this had increased to eleven, more than a quarter of the forty-strong class. Harlech Castle stands on the Harlech dome which is at the end of the Rinog mountains; when built the sea lapped around it but it is now several hundred yards inland. It dated back to the reign of Edward I in the 13th century and went through numerous periods of turbulence over the years. Owen Glendower captured it in 1404 but it fell five years later and led to his defeat. It was the last refuge of the Lancastrians in the area during 1468. Two centuries later Harlech was the last Royalist castle in Wales before it was captured by Parliamentary forces.

Penrhyndeudraeth

The three people sitting on the bench framed by the Penrhyndeudraeth running-in board are the photographer's wife and two companions. Hence, they were not about to join the train as '90XX' 4-4-0 No. 9003 waits with a Barmouth to Pwllheli train before setting off on the steep 1 in 65 climb towards Minffordd in the early 1950s. It was built in July 1936 from 'Bulldog' No. 3424 and 'Duke' No. 3275 as No. 3203 and carried the name *Earl Cawdor* until June 1937; it was renumbered to 9003 in July 1946. No. 9003 was allocated to Oswestry, working on the Whitchurch to Aberystwyth route, until its transfer to Machynlleth in 1949. By 1953 the 'Manor' 4-6-0s had taken took over the heavier passenger duties on the Cambrian and Nos. 9000-9003 were included in the Western Region's 1954 Condemnation Programme. They were taken out of service in 1954/5 with No. 9003 the last to go, in October 1955, even though it was noted under repair in Oswestry Works in April of that year. To the right of the coaches are some of the buildings of Cooke's Explosives factory, the main industry not just in Penrhyndeudraeth but in the surrounding area. The company manufactured gelignite, mainly for the coal mining industry, from its seventy acre site and provided a considerable amount of traffic for the railway. Note the covered steps at the end of the signal box to give protection from the gales which swept up the Traeth Bach estuary from the Irish Sea; in front is the signalman's bicycle propped up against the wooden fence.

T.G. Hepburn/Rail Archive Stephenson

CHAPTER 4 - MORFA MAWDDACH (BARMOUTH JUNCTION) TO PWLLHELI

BR Standard Class '3' 2-6-2T No. 82020 at Penrhyndeudraeth on a southbound train, probably in 1964. It was at Machynlleth from March 1960 and remained on the Cambrian until May 1965 when it left for Nine Elms. No. 82020 was in unlined green with a large BR emblem from July 1961 onwards.

Minffordd

'4575' 2-6-2T No. 5510 on the 1 in 50 approaching Minffordd with the Up 'Cambrian Coast Express' on 18th May 1959. It had only arrived at Machynlleth the previous month from Swindon where it had been allocated since 1941; No. 5510 was withdrawn in February 1961. The five coaches from Pwllheli will join those from Aberystwyth at Dovey Junction for the journey to Paddington. Garth Quarry on the right was opened in 1870 with production focused on the extraction of dolerite which produces a high-specification aggregate used for road surfacing and railway ballast; it is still in operation today.

Peter W. Gray/Rail Archive Stephenson

CHAPTER 4 - MORFA MAWDDACH (BARMOUTH JUNCTION) TO PWLLHELI

Minffordd was the summit of the climb from Penrhyndeudraeth, and the line then descended immediately at 1 in 50 towards Portmadoc as is clear from '45XX' 2-6-2T No. 4549 arriving at the station with a train from Portmadoc on 16th May 1959. The 'Prairie' was built in 1915 and originally worked in Devon and Cornwall until 1937 when it arrived at Machynlleth; No. 4549 returned to the south west in February 1960 for its final years in service up to withdrawal at the end of 1961. Although the line through Minffordd opened in October 1867 no station was provided at first, although it was where the Cambrian Railways' coastal line met the Ffestiniog Railway. The narrow gauge line had been carrying slate from quarries at Blaenau Ffestiniog to Portmadoc Harbour since 1836 and exchange sidings with the Cambrian were opened there. In 1872 new passenger stations at Minffordd were added to the timetables of both companies. The Cambrian station had a single curved platform with a simple wooden shelter and no passing loop. Although the signal cabin on the right had nineteen levers, it is lettered 'MINFFORDD GROUND FRAME'. The open wagon at the end of the slate siding has had two end planks replaced by metal channel – this was less susceptible to damage from shifting loads but here appears to be delivering sand or possibly lime, which is being off-loaded on the offside. Unsurprisingly, given the nearby quarry, the ballast in the station and sidings is immaculate.

Peter W. Gray/Rail Archive Stephenson

With Garth Quarry in the background '2251' 0-6-0 No. 2294 approaches Minffordd station with the 10.25am Pwllheli to Barmouth train on 9th September 1961. It was transferred to Machynlleth from Croes Newydd in October 1959 and was withdrawn a year after this picture was taken.
M.J. Fox/Rail Archive Stephenson

BR Standard Class '3' 2-6-2T No. 82020 arrives at Minffordd with the 3.45pm Barmouth-Pwllheli on 18th June 1962. It was at Machynlleth from March 1960 until April 1965 when it went to the Southern Region at Nine Elms for use on the Waterloo Empty Coaching Stock work. It had been repainted from its original lined black into lined green in 1958 but lost the lining on its next repaint in July 1961. The bridge in the background carries both the A497 road from Nefyn to Penrhyndeudraeth via Pwllheli, Criccieth and Portmadoc and the tracks of the Festiniog Railway line. This had re-opened from Portmadoc to Minffordd in 1956, the first section of the line restored by the preservationists. No. 82020 has come up the steep 1 in 65 gradient on the line from Penrhyndeudraeth, which is highlighted by the height difference from the siding on the right holding shock-absorbing wagons, which was level.

CHAPTER 4 - MORFA MAWDDACH (BARMOUTH JUNCTION) TO PWLLHELI

BR Standard Class '3' 2-6-2T No. 82020 arrives at Minffordd with the 4.5pm train from Pwllheli on 9th September 1961. Note the Shock wagons for the slate traffic which from the closure of the Festiniog Railway in 1946 was brought in by road from Blaenau Ffestiniog to the exchange sidings at Minffordd. The sidings are currently being restored by the Ffestiniog & Welsh Highland Railways Trust. The sign on the end of the waiting room directs passengers to the Festiniog Railway station, reached via a short footpath. Minffordd was the nearest station to the famous village of Portmeirion, a mile away. It was designed and built by Sir Clough Williams-Ellis between 1925 and 1975 in the style of an Italian village and is now owned by a charitable trust. *Mike Fox/Rail Archive Stephenson*

'2251' 0-6-0 No. 3200 has just crossed the Glaslyn Bridge on the eastern approach to Portmadoc with the 1.38pm Dovey Junction to Pwllheli train on 9th September 1961. It was built in 1946 and at this date was allocated to Oswestry, moving to Templecombe on the Somerset & Dorset in 1963. The Afon Glaslyn was about sixteen miles long and flowed from the Glaslyn Lake on the slopes of Snowdon before passing through the tidal sluices on the Cob at the south-eastern end of Portmadoc and into Tremadog Bay. *M.J. Fox/Rail Archive Stephenson*

On the same day, BR Standard Class '3' 2-6-2T No. 82033 and a Collett '2251' 0-6-0 cross the bridge in the other direction with the 9.45am Pwllheli to Paddington train. The line here was just 24ft above sea level. No. 82033 was transferred from Bristol Barrow Road to Machynlleth at the end of 1960 and worked on the Cambrian until mid-1964. *M.J. Fox/Rail Archive Stephenson*

Portmadoc

Portmadoc developed as a slate-shipping port and later became a holiday resort. The station was just 24 feet above sea level where the line crossed the estuary of Afon Glaslyn.

Pedestrians wait at the level crossing for BR Standard Class '2' 2-6-0 No. 78000 as it arrives at Portmadoc with the Down 'Cambrian Coast Express' to Pwllheli, probably in 1954. The first ten of the class went initially to Oswestry but Nos. 78000-7 were there for only a short time and moved to Machynlleth; No. 78000 was transferred there in April 1953 and stayed until in May 1963 when it moved to Nottingham. The 2-6-0s worked between Shrewsbury, Oswestry and the Cambrian Coast including the Aberystwyth and Pwllheli portions of the newly renamed 'Cambrian Coast Express' in summer 1954, taking it through to Shrewsbury. However, they struggled to cope when the train loaded to more than seven coaches and 'Manor' 4-6-0s and '43XX' 2-6-0s took over from the start of the winter timetable. On the left is a small cattle dock and loading bay; the main goods facilities were at the west end of the station.

A close-up view of '90XX' 4-4-0 No. 9014 as it waits for the level crossing gates to be opened before departing down the coast to Barmouth. The outside frames, large dome and tall chimney were reminiscent of a much older engine than one which only entered service in 1937. Although lined out in 1949, by the date of this picture No. 9014 was in plain black and has fluted coupling rods and a later type of superheated boiler with top feed; several of the class had three or four different boilers over their working lives. The cab side sheets were set outward at the back to suit the larger Dean and Churchward tenders. Note the weather sheet complete with its tensioning springs tied back on the cab roof.

'90XX' 4-4-0 No. 9004 at Portmadoc with an Up local probably the 1.55pm from Pwllheli, in September 1958. No. 9004 was at Machynlleth from before nationalisation, moving to Croes Newydd in June 1957 and was one of the last of the class remaining in service when withdrawn in June 1960. Built in August 1936 from the frames of 'Bulldog' No. 3439 and 'Duke' No. 3271, it was named *Earl of Dartmouth* until June 1937 when the name was removed and used on newly built 'Castle' No. 5047. In their final years the 'Dukedogs' spent the winter in store and only returned for the Summer Timetable. *The Railway Observer* noted No. 9004 several times between 1957 and 1959. 'Nos. 9004/14 from Croes Newydd shed, which acquired them *for the summer of 1957*, were also in evidence. On Saturdays one would usually assist an 0-6-0 throughout on the 11.0 a.m. Ruabon-Pwllheli, spend *a week in the area, then return to Ruabon the following Saturday as assistant on the 7.20 a.m. Pwllheli-Paddington'.* In August 1958, '9004 was observed working local passenger and goods trains between Portmadoc and Pwllheli … *including the 1.55pm Pwllheli-Portmadoc and the 6.0pm Afon Wen-Portmadoc on 16th August'.* In 1959 it is noted that No. 9004 was 'considered by one driver to be the best of the surviving Dukedogs' and it was recorded working between Ruabon and Pwllheli and between Barmouth and Pwllheli. Portmadoc Signal Box on the left was a Dutton 'Type 2' box built by the Cambrian Railways in March 1894 as Portmadoc East. In 1932 the GWR extended the lever frame from fourteen to thirty-eight levers and the length of the corresponding building to accommodate it when Portmadoc West box was abolished; the 'East' designation was dropped at this date. The extension is evident in this view with different brickwork beyond the nameboard. The box lasted until the installation of Radio Electric Token Block signalling and closed in October 1988.

Stephen Summerson/Rail Archive Stephenson

CHAPTER 4 - MORFA MAWDDACH (BARMOUTH JUNCTION) TO PWLLHELI

The pictures on the following three pages were probably taken by Kenneth Field on a visit to Portmadoc during May or June 1959 although it is likely that he made more than one visit during the year based on the shed allocations of the engines he photographed.

BR Standard Class '4' 4-6-0 No. 75020 arrives at Portmadoc with 'The North Wales Radio Land Cruise' train from Pwllheli going south along the Cambrian Coast line, before it was fitted with a double chimney and repainted green in November 1959. Its 89C shedplate shows that this picture was taken after Nos. 75020 and 75026 had been transferred from Tyseley in June 1959 to assist with the Cambrian line summer holiday traffic. They were noted on the 'North Wales Radio Land Cruise' which took holidaymakers from Pwllheli to Rhyl via Corwen returning through Llandudno and Caernarvon on a tour of the scenic splendours of Snowdonia.
Kenneth Field/Rail Archive Stephenson

The shunter clings onto the cab handrail as he stands on the footstep of '2251' 0-6-0 No. 2294 shunting its pick-up goods train which it will leave in the platform as it offloads or adds wagons. Portmadoc was an important place for goods traffic, hence the large goods shed on the right.
Kenneth Field/Rail Archive Stephenson

Following from the picture on the previous page, No. 2294 has detached several wagons, picked up an empty tank and rejoined its train. The shunter has coupled it up and stands back to wait for No. 2294 to set off for Pwllheli. The Collett '2251' 0-6-0 was allocated to Machynlleth for its last three years in service, moving there from Croes Newydd in October 1959. *Kenneth Field/Rail Archive Stephenson*

CHAPTER 4 - MORFA MAWDDACH (BARMOUTH JUNCTION) TO PWLLHELI

'4575' 2-6-2T No. 5553 arrives at Portmadoc with a Class '9' goods train from Pwllheli. It had been transferred from Bristol Bath Road in December 1958 and was at Machynlleth for two years, until December 1960. On the right of the picture is the two-road engine shed which under British Railways became a sub-shed of Machynlleth with six or seven engines, usually a couple of 2-6-2Ts and '2251' 0-6-0s, stabled there overnight every day in the early 1950s. Their duties included banking/piloting over Minffordd summit, local goods trains to Barmouth and Pwllheli and passenger trains to Pwllheli and Machynlleth. Note the shed windows are covered with mesh, presumably to protect them from stones falling from wagons freshly loaded at Garth Quarry. *Kenneth Field/Rail Archive Stephenson*

Churchward '43XX' 2-6-0 No. 6340 rolls into a busy Portmadoc with a summer Saturday express from the Midlands to Pwllheli. It was at Stourbridge Junction from June 1957 until January 1961 when it was transferred to Plymouth Laira. Until 1957 the coastal route north of Barmouth had a 'Yellow' classification and after it was raised to 'Blue' this allowed the use of larger engines, 'Manor' 4-6-0s, '43XX' 2-6-0s and BR Standard Class '4' 4-6-0s, on the heavier trains through to Pwllheli.

Kenneth Field/Rail Archive Stephenson

Stanier Class '3' 2-6-2T No. 40085 runs in with a train for Pwllheli as the 'North Wales Radio Land Cruise train', headed by No. 75020 in the earlier picture, stands in the adjacent platform. The LM&SR-designed tank was allocated to Wrexham Rhosddu, which became 84K in February 1958, from late-1956 until January 1960 when it moved to Machynlleth.

Kenneth Field/Rail Archive Stephenson

CHAPTER 4 - MORFA MAWDDACH (BARMOUTH JUNCTION) TO PWLLHELI

The Collett '2251' 0-6-0s worked both freight and passenger trains along the Cambrian Coast. No. 2271 waits at Portmadoc with an eastbound local, shortly before it left Machynlleth for Neyland in May 1959. The large water tower supplied columns at the outer end of both the Up and Down platforms in addition to those at the engine shed.
Kenneth Field/ Rail Archive Stephenson

'2251' 0-6-0 No. 2294 shunting a Down pick-up goods at the west end of Portmadoc. This picture from the footbridge was taken after No. 2294 had moved to Machynlleth from Oswestry in October 1959. In the background are the goods sidings and carriage sidings curving round following the line towards Criccieth and Pwllheli.
Kenneth Field/Rail Archive Stephenson

BR Standard Class '3' 2-6-2T No. 82006 with a Down Class 'E' freight, the first vehicle of which is a loaded 20T Loco Coal wagon for either Portmadoc or Pwllheli shed. This picture was taken after it had been transferred to Machynlleth in February 1961. It was there for over four years, ending its days at Nine Elms from April 1965 until withdrawn in September 1966.
Kenneth Field/Rail Archive Stephenson

A view from the footbridge looking west; all three engines in the picture are BR Standard designs which by this date, 18th August 1962, had ousted most of the GWR engines from the Cambrian Coast lines. A Class '3' 2-6-2T departs for Criccieth and Pwllheli, Class '2' 2-6-0 No. 78007 is in the goods yard and a Class '4' 4-6-0 is in the carriage sidings.

CHAPTER 4 - MORFA MAWDDACH (BARMOUTH JUNCTION) TO PWLLHELI

'2251' 0-6-0 No. 3208 was at Oswestry from new in 1946. It moved to Machynlleth in June 1963 and was withdrawn there in August 1965; it has no shedplate so probably was newly transferred. The sub-shed at Portmadoc had closed in August 1963 though both the carriage and goods sidings remain in use. By this date former GWR engines had all but disappeared and been replaced by BR Standard or LM&SR types: during a two week period in June only a single '2251' was noted north of Barmouth.

BR Standard Class '3' 2-6-2T No. 82032 arrives from Pwllheli with a long Class 'E' goods on 25th July 1963. It entered service at the start of 1955 and by the time it was transferred to Machynlleth in August 1961 it had already been allocated to eight different sheds. It stayed only four months before moving to Shrewsbury although it would return a year later. It was destined to have a working life of a little over ten years, being withdrawn in April 1965 from Bangor. There are six fitted vans at the front of the train, hence the Class 'E' headlamps, followed by a GWR 'Toad' brake van which is unlikely to be fitted but may be 'through piped'.

Brian Stephenson

The signalman hands over the single line token for the section to Barmouth before BR Standard Class '3' 2-6-2T No. 82032 leaves Portmadoc with its goods train on 25th July 1963. The track to Barmouth ran in a straight line for some distance before turning to the right to follow the coast. The first three 12-ton vans in the train are of late LM&SR design and have large sliding doors, the first two being No. M524504 with plywood sides and No. M508393 with planked sides; they have pasted labels indicating animal feeds have been recently carried.
Brian Stephenson

Black Rock

'2251' 0-6-0 No. 2232 heads past a stormy and almost deserted Tremadoc Bay at Black Rock, to the east of Criccieth, on a westbound train to Pwllheli in around 1957. No. 2232 had been a Shrewsbury engine in the mid-1950s but had moved to Machynlleth in March 1956. It was there for slightly less than five years, leaving for Bristol St. Philip's Marsh in February 1961.

'43XX' 2-6-0 No. 6378 approaching Black Rock Halt between Portmadoc and Criccieth on 25th July 1963. It was one of thirty-five of the class built by Robert Stephenson & Co. for the Great Western Railway in 1920/21; it was never fitted with outside steam pipes. No. 6378 was at Shrewsbury for four months then went to Machynlleth from June 1956 until August 1963.
Brian Stephenson

Cricceith

Half a dozen of the then remaining eleven 'Duke' 4-4-0s had worked alongside the '90XX' 4-4-0s on the Cambrian during the Second World War and No. 9054 *Cornubia* was one of the last four in service. In its final year it worked passenger trains from Machynlleth on both the Aberystwyth and Pwllheli lines and was on one of the latter when photographed half a mile east of Criccieth station at Merllyn Crossing with a train from Pwllheli. It was built in 1895 as No. 3255 and was withdrawn in June 1950 leaving the remaining three of the class; one went in December 1950 and the final two in April and July 1951.

'Dean Goods' 0-6-0 No. 2464 shunting a horsebox at Criccieth, probably in 1948. The three surviving Machynlleth-based engines in the class were observed working the daily pick-up goods between Portmadoc and Machynlleth at this time. No. 2464 was the first of the three to be taken out of traffic when it was withdrawn in December 1949 having clocked up almost fifty-four years in service. They had been staple power on Cambrian freight services since the mid-1920s. The horsebox is of London, Brighton & South Coast Railway origin and is very similar to the more common London & South Western Railway design, but with a tighter radius on the roof profile. It had been updated in Southern Railway days to their 'house style' by replacing panelling with metal sheet and adding curved metal door bangers; the Southern never built any new horseboxes.

'90XX' 4-4-0 No. 9017 near Merllyn Crossing, half a mile east of Criccieth station, heading an eastbound train towards Portmadoc. The 'Dukedogs' were built between 1936 and 1939 and were technically a rebuild of the 'Bulldog' Class 4-4-0s (using their frames) to produce a replacement for the 'Duke' Class 4-4-0s. Six years earlier 'Duke' No. 3265 *Tre Pol and Pen* was rebuilt on the frames of 'Bulldog' No. 3365 *Charles Grey Mott* and within a few months of emerging from Swindon it went to Oswestry where it stayed until withdrawal as No. 9065 in December 1949. The first five of the new engines followed it to the Cambrian, working between Whitchurch and Aberystwyth and from Machynlleth to Pwllheli. In 1939, eighteen of the thirty engines rebuilt (including No. 3265) were allocated to either Oswestry, Machynlleth or Aberystwyth and by 1947 this had increased to twenty. Up to the War the class was used almost exclusively on passenger work but by the end of the War were increasingly used as mixed traffic engines after the Cambrian main line had been upgraded to 'Blue' status which allowed '43XX' 2-6-0s and 'Manors' to be used. By 1953 'Manors' had taken over all of their heavier Cambrian duties and three of the Cambrian engines were withdrawn in 1954/5 and others went into store, especially during the winter months. In summer 1957, fifteen were withdrawn followed by two at the end of 1958, one in July 1959 and the final five between June and October 1960.

One of the last of the class to be condemned, in October 1960, No. 9017 was the subject of the first-ever appeal for funds to purchase a standard gauge locomotive for preservation, with the intention of it being preserved on the Bluebell Railway (the only suitable home for it in 1961). It was kept in store at Oswestry Works through 1961, to give time for the funds to be raised. The appeal did not reach its target and Peter Gomm (of enamel badge fame), with assistance from Peter Summers (who also covered the cost of transport to the Bluebell), stepped in to fund the difference between what was raised and the asking price, and then placed the locomotive on permanent loan to the Bluebell Railway. It has since been donated to the Bluebell, with the requirement that it is to remain normally on that Railway. When built as No. 3217, it had been allocated the name *Earl of Berkeley*, but never carried it having been built in March 1938, the year after the names were taken off the rebuilt engines in June/July 1937. Instead the name was used on 'Castle' No. 5060 but since 1965 No. 9017 has carried *Earl of Berkeley* plates.

The rear of the train has just passed over the crossing which leads down to the Esplanade along the sea front at Criccieth. The large building on the left with 'Café' in bold capital letters is the Morannedd Café building designed by the famous architect Clough Williams Ellis. It was built in 1954 and has a distinctive curved shape, with floor-to-ceiling windows overlooking the sea which resulted in it receiving Grade II listing status in 1994 as *'A distinctive sea-side pavillion which is a rare essay in the International modern style by one of the leading Welsh architects of the twentieth century'*. One of its early owners was Sir William 'Billy' Butlin and holidaymakers would be brought in by bus from the nearby Butlin's holiday camp to attend Tea Dances. After the Butlin's era ended, the building was rented to various tenants over the years and in 2015 Dylan's Restaurant took over the building and it underwent extensive refurbishment.

A family waits at the level crossing gates for BR Standard Class '3' 2-6-2T No. 82032 to depart down the hill towards Portmadoc in 1961. Note the standard GWR 'short' trespass sign with its 'Great Western Railway' heading overpainted.

BR Standard Class '3' 2-6-2T No. 82020 at Criccieth with a train to Pwllheli, probably in 1963. No. 82020 was originally intended for the North Eastern Region but instead went to Nuneaton on the London Midland Region where there was a temporary shortage of motive power for local passenger work. It moved to the Western Region at Wrexham Rhosddu in October 1956 and to Machynlleth in March 1960.

Afon Wen

The station was in an isolated location about half-a-mile south of Afon Wen on the edge of the Irish Sea, east of the junction with the Carnarvon Railway's line from Menai Bridge. In July 1870 the latter became part of the L&NWR and by 1871, after the opening of the line through Caernarvon, the L&NWR was running trains between Afon Wen and Bangor. Afon Wen had three platform faces, two on an island platform which housed the main station building. There were two footbridges, one at each end. By the 1930s Wales had become a popular holiday destination, and here during the summer months there were over one hundred train movements each day, especially since trains from the LM&SR line had to reverse there for their return journey. To service their locomotives, two water tanks were provided together with several areas for clinker and ash disposal.

After the opening of Butlin's Holiday Camp nearby in 1947 traffic in the summer months increased considerably since most visitors arrived by rail. The platforms at the eastern end of the station were lengthened to take up to twelve-coach trains. The Afon Wen-Menai Bridge line was closed in December 1964 under the Beeching Plan, including Afon Wen station itself, although the signal box remained in use until April 1967.

There is plenty of activity on the island platform as passengers leave the express on the left, probably to wait for the next train to Penychain and Butlin's Holiday Camp, in June 1956. The local service from that direction is headed by '4575' 2-6-2T No. 5507. The 'Prairie' tank was at Machynlleth from April 1947 until withdrawn in August 1958.

With Tremadoc Bay on the right, '90XX' 4-4-0 No. 9021 arrives at Afon Wen with a train for Pwllheli in June 1957. It was always on the Cambrian at Machynlleth or its Aberystwyth sub-shed until withdrawn in December 1958, although it had been in store from much of 1956 onwards, emerging only for the summer timetable. *The Railway Observer* noted it working for several weeks on the Up 'Cambrian Coast Express' from Pwllheli to Dovey Junction, returning with empty stock to Barmouth and then taking the 3.40pm Barmouth-Pwllheli. No. 9021 has a later pattern of boiler with top feed but reverted to the earlier type in April 1958. It was built in November 1938 from the boiler, cab and fittings of 'Duke' No. 3259 *Merlin* combined with the frames from 'Bulldog' No. 3411. No. 9021 was the second engine of Lot 331 which was for twenty engines but only nine were completed when the Second World War broke out; these had new boilers unlike the earlier engines which had secondhand 'Duke' boilers.

The fireman of Collett '2251' 0-6-0 No. 2204 has a breather while waiting for the signals at Afon Wen in 1960 or 1961. There were carriage sidings on both sides of the line at the east end of the station. No. 2204 was at Machynlleth from before nationalisation until June 1962 when it went to Templecombe on the Somerset & Dorset.
Kenneth Field/Rail Archive Stephenson

Another '2251' waits with an eastbound freight at Afon Wen because the signal is off for the Fairburn 2-6-4T to run out towards the carriage sidings past the other LM&SR 2-6-4T waiting there.
Kenneth Field/Rail Archive Stephenson

CHAPTER 4 - MORFA MAWDDACH (BARMOUTH JUNCTION) TO PWLLHELI

'2251' 0-6-0 No. 2271 has just arrived at Afon Wen's Platform 2 with a train from Pwllheli, probably in 1958, during the time it was at Machynlleth between July 1954 and May 1959. Unusually and a reflection of the requirements on busy summer Saturdays, Afon Wen had two water towers to supply the many engines which brought in trains which terminated there, especially when the nearby Butlin's Pwllheli Holiday Camp was at its peak.
Kenneth Field/Rail Archive Stephenson

The island platform at Afon Wen handled trains on both the Up Main (Platform 2) and also the Up passenger loop (Platform 3) where Stanier Class '3' 2-6-2T No. 40086 is waiting with a train from Pwllheli in 1960. No. 40086 was transferred to Machynlleth from Wrexham Rhosddu in January of that year but only stayed until November.

Kenneth Field/Rail Archive Stephenson

The weekday London Midland Region passenger trains from the North Wales coast over the line from Menai Bridge were worked for over a decade by Ivatt Class '2' 2-6-2Ts. No. 41276 heads away from Afon Wen towards Pwllheli in around 1957 while a Stanier 2-6-2T fills its tanks on what was known as the 'Ash Road'. No. 41276 was allocated to Rhyl from new in October 1950 until December 1962 when it left for the Southern Region at Brighton. The usual London Midland Region motive power for most of their workings along the line from Caernarvon were the tank engines of Fowler, Stanier or Fairburn design.

Penychain

With part of the Butlin's Pwllheli Holiday Camp on the right '43XX' No. 6395 leaves Penychain with a train from Pwllheli in 1962. It was built for the GWR by Robert Stephenson & Co., entering service in December 1921, and was at Machynlleth from June 1960 until October 1962. The station originally opened as a halt in July 1933, one of several added by the Great Western in the 1920s and 1930s, making the average distance between stations over the 53¼ miles between Dovey Junction and Pwllheli line just 1½ miles. Butlin's built the camp in 1940 for the Admiralty to serve as HMS Glendower, a Royal Navy training base and after the War ended it was opened in March 1947 as Butlin's holiday camp and the halt was upgraded to a station to cater for what became a high volume of traffic over the next two decades. The Rank Organisation took over Butlin's in 1972 and the camp was extensively modernised in the 1990s. It was transferred to Butlin's sister company, Haven Holidays, in 1998 and is now owned by Bourne Leisure; today it operates under the name Hafyn-y-môr Holiday Park. Behind the photographer, the railway divided the Holiday Camp into two halves. A single-span over-bridge from where this picture was taken connected the South Camp to the West, Middle, and East Camp areas which were located to the north of the railway on the right of this picture.

Pwllheli

Pwllheli is the terminus of the coastal route from Dovey Junction. Its first station was opened in 1867 on the eastern edge of the town at Glan-y-don. After the harbour there silted up a new one was constructed to the south, releasing land that enabled Cambrian Railways to build a half mile extension to a new terminus adjacent to the town centre and this opened in July 1907; the original station became a goods depot. The new terminus had a single island platform with engine release roads on either side. During 1923 the GWR doubled the last mile of the approach track and improved the station with new canopies.

BR Standard Class '3' 2-6-2T No. 82005 pulls into Pwllheli, probably in 1964. It was on the Cambrian, allocated to Machynlleth between November 1961 and April 1965, when it left to spend its last four months in service at Nine Elms.

BR Standard Class '2' 2-6-0 No. 78002 awaits departure from Pwllheli with the 5.25pm to Barmouth in 1957. One of the first ten of the class which went initially to Oswestry when they emerged from Darlington Works in late 1952 and early 1953, No. 78002 left for Machynlleth in May 1953 and stayed there for a decade until it moved to Wigan Central shed. By the summer of 1957, following bridge strengthening, the coastal section from Dovey Junction to Barmouth Junction and Portmadoc was cleared for larger engines although the Class '2' 2-6-0s continued working lighter duties on the route. There was a locomotive depot, a sub-shed of Machynlleth, situated alongside the goods depot, and four engines were regularly stabled there each night. Two Class '2' 2-6-0s were regularly sub-shedded there; the sub-shed allocations were changed every few days. The shed was modernised with a new two road building in 1959 to replace the 1907 Cambrian Railways single road shed but was in use for only seven years after DMUs replaced steam on the Cambrian Coast line. Note the starter signal which is still of Cambrian Railways' origin and lacks a decorative finial.

5 – Barmouth Junction to Dovey Junction

The line which followed the coast from Barmouth via Towyn and Aberdovey to Dovey Junction had been authorised by the Aberystwith [sic] & Welsh Coast Railway and was completed under the Cambrian Railways in 1867.

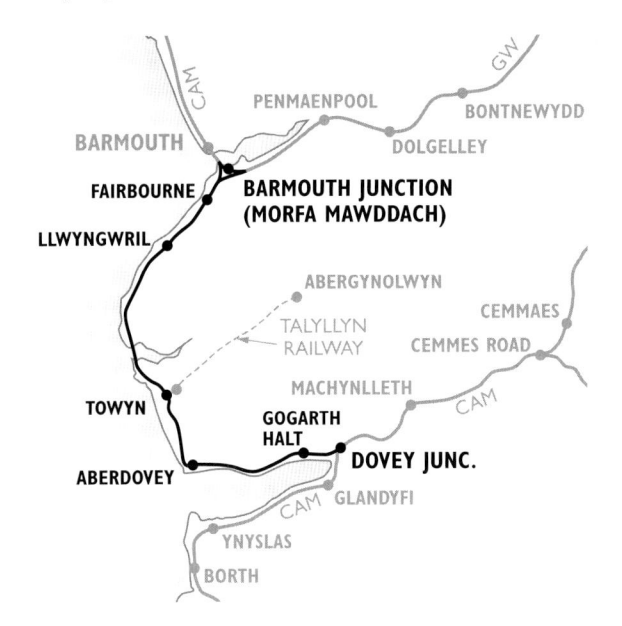

Fairbourne

The lady in the Camping Coach on the right who has hung her washing out to dry between the end of the coach and the fence on the platform, watches as '2251' 0-6-0 No. 2289 prepares to depart from Fairbourne to Barmouth in 1957. No. 2289 was allocated to Oxford until transferred to Oswestry in April 1956 and then moved on to Machynlleth three months later; it returned to Oxford in December 1957. Fairbourne station dated back to June 1899, replacing the former Barmouth Ferry station which closed in 1867 when the Barmouth bridge was opened. The tall building at this end of the station is the station master's house and the canopy beyond is on the station building. The Camping Coaches were introduced by the GWR in 1934 with three of them going to Central Wales and six to the Cambrian Coast; more were added in 1935. When they were restored after the Second World War in 1952 the number in use in the whole of the Western Region totalled seventy coaches. On the Cambrian they were maintained at Aberdovey in a converted concrete shed and store. The coach at Fairbourne is on its own length of track next to the goods siding which remained in use until 1964.

Llwyngwril

The driver watches while the fireman climbs round the running plate of BR Standard Class '3' 2-6-2T No. 82003 on a northbound train as it takes on water at Llwyngwril, probably in 1964 after Machynlleth became 6F in September 1963. It had been transferred there from Carmarthen in June 1962 and stayed until March 1965. No. 82003 had been painted in lined green livery during overhaul at Swindon Works in May 1957. This was the longer platform, extended in 1909, with the station building on the shorter Up platform, which ended in steps rather than a ramp. The GWR pattern water column was supplied from a 25,000 gallon tank installed in 1937, at what was a rather remote location, to replace a small 4,000 gallon Cambrian Railways' tank; there was a similar column at the other end of the station.

Tyseley's No. 7823 *Hook Norton Manor* waits to pass a southbound train at Llwyngwril while heading an express to Barmouth and Pwllheli. The 'Manor' had been in Cornwall from 1955 until its transfer to Machynlleth in April 1959, staying until November 1962 when it moved to Tyseley. With no footbridge, passengers changing platforms were required to use the wooden walkway in front of *Hook Norton Manor*. The vehicle visible to the left of the train in the background in the siding at the end of the Up platform is the Camping Coach which was still in use until at least 1969.

At the Barmouth end of the station there was an occupation level crossing unprotected by gates or signals which BR Standard Class '4' 2-6-4T No. 80098 is passing over as it arrives at Llwyngwril in 1963. No. 80098 was on the London, Tilbury & Southend from new in December 1954 until July 1962 when it was displaced by electrification and moved to Old Oak Common for storage, then Shrewsbury in September and on to Croes Newydd in November and finally to Machynlleth in March 1963. It was rescued from Barry scrapyard and is based at the Midland Railway Centre at Butterley; it is currently (2020) undergoing a Heavy General overhaul and has been out of ticket since 2009 having been restored for main line operation in 1998.

Towyn

Cambrian Railways 0-6-0 No. 844 is sandwiched between a GWR 12-ton van and a Stephenson Clarke former Private Owner coal wagon, now in British Railways' ownership, while shunting at Towyn on 20th August 1953. It was a 'Large Belpaire Goods' or Class '15', intended for use over the whole system except for the Mid-Wales line. The fifteen engines were the last 0-6-0s built for the Cambrian Railways and the first Cambrian engines to be built with Belpaire fireboxes. They were rebuilt by the GWR in the 1920s and 1930s with new boilers and GWR standard fittings such as the 'coffee-pot' safety valve covers. No. 844 was the first of the final batch of five built by the Manchester locomotive builders Beyer, Peacock & Co. Ltd in late-1918, although ordered in January 1915. It was originally Cambrian Railways No. 15 and was withdrawn from Oswestry in August 1954, having ended its days as a stationary boiler at Oswestry Works.

'2251' 0-6-0 No. 2292 has just left Towyn working a train towards Dovey Junction on 19th August 1954. It was allocated to Tyseley from before nationalisation until November 1952 except for a few months at Machynlleth in mid-1952. It returned to Wales at Croes Newydd in July 1954 for three months before moving to Severn Tunnel Junction where it remained until withdrawal in June 1962.

On the left of this picture – which was taken from the Neptune Road Bridge looking back towards the station – is a refuge siding which had a short platform once used by the Phoenix Tramway which conveyed building materials to the seafront, and in the right background is the goods yard and goods shed.

CHAPTER 5 - BARMOUTH JUNCTION TO DOVEY JUNCTION

The fireman of '2251' 0-6-0 No. 2202 has just collected the token for the single line section to Barmouth Junction and the signalman at Towyn walks back with the token for the section from Aberdovey to the GWR built signal box which had replaced the two earlier Cambrian Railways' boxes in 1923. There were no token set-down or pick-up posts on the Up line and only a setting-down post on the Down line; low platforms were provided on each side for the signalman. No. 2202 was at Croes Newydd for three months in 1955 before moving to Banbury in October. It came to the Cambrian in March 1956, first at Machynlleth, then Oswestry in January 1959 and finally back to Machynlleth the following month; it was an early withdrawal in October 1960. This picture was taken from the station footbridge looking south towards Dovey Junction with the goods yard on the left containing half a dozen cattle wagons. The tall shed furthest from the camera is the goods shed, next is the cement storage shed and on the left the prefabricated building is for grain storage; all three were served by the same siding. A considerable amount of slate traffic was once brought in by the 2ft 3in. gauge Talyllyn Railway from quarries near Abergynolwyn to a wharf just beyond the Neptune Road bridge in the distance. The backdrop to this picture is provided by Graig Fach-goch on the left and Llechwedd Melyn and Foel Caethle to the right.

The signal has been pulled off to allow BR Standard Class '3' 2-6-2T No. 82020 to enter the single line section to Morfa Mawddach in the early 1960s. It was built at Swindon Works in September 1954, the first of ten engines in Lot 398 which were originally allocated to the North Eastern Region, but instead No. 82020 went to Nuneaton on the London Midland Region where there was a temporary shortage of motive power for local passenger work. It moved to the Western Region at Wrexham Rhosddu in October 1956 and to Machynlleth in March 1960. No. 82020 was withdrawn from Nine Elms in September 1965, less than six months after leaving the Cambrian. In the background is the pre-cast concrete footbridge, unique on the Cambrian system, which in 1935 replaced the previous wooden bridge. There was originally a small wooden waiting shelter on the northbound platform, but it was removed in 1961. The GWR tubular post signal dates from the mid-1930s; note the square contact box attached to the rear of the post immediately below the finial.

In lined black livery, unlike most of its classmates which had been repainted in green, BR Standard Class '3' 2-6-2T No. 82000 heads a lengthy Up goods near Towyn on 19th April 1963. It was a Western Region engine from new in 1952 and reached the Cambrian at Machynlleth in January 1960 after eleven months at Wrexham Rhosddu.
D.M.C. Hepburne-Scott/Rail Archive Stephenson

No. 7801 *Anthony Manor* near Towyn with a Pwllheli to Machynlleth train conveying a 12T van at the rear on 18th April 1963. It was built in 1938 as part of the GWR's replacement of its older '43XX' 2-6-0s, incorporating their wheels and motion, and was originally to be named *Ashley Manor* but received the name intended for No. 7800 which was given the name *Torquay Manor*. No. 7801 was at Oswestry from autumn 1958 until 1963 when the five 'Manors' there went to Shrewsbury following the transfer of the Cambrian lines to the London Midland Region.
D.M.C. Hepburne-Scott/Rail Archive Stephenson

Aberdovey

Above: Slightly further along the estuary, the now-preserved BR Standard Class '4' 2-6-4T No. 80098 heads a Machynlleth to Barmouth train on 18th April 1963. It was on the London, Tilbury & Southend from new in December 1954 until that line was electrified in July 1962; it was transferred to Machynlleth from Croes Newydd in March 1963. *D.M.C. Hepburne-Scott/Rail Archive Stephenson*

Right: Machynlleth BR Standard Class '3' 2-6-2T No. 82020 approaching Aberdovey as it skirts the estuary of the River Dovey heading west towards Morfa Mawddach in the early 1960s. Jutting out on the right is Picnic Island, a misnomer, because it was actually a small peninsula separated from the 'mainland' after being cut off by the railway in 1863.

The photographers at Aberdovey station and a BR Standard Class '4' 4-6-0 wait for No. 82020 to arrive from Dovey Junction, probably in late 1964 or early 1965 before it was transferred to Nine Elms.

Gogarth Halt

Above: Gogarth Halt was about 1½ miles west of Dovey Junction and was built on marshland at the edge of the Dovey Estuary. It was opened in July 1923, over twenty years after the first proposals were made and had a 99ft-long wooden platform and small waiting shed. BR Standard Class '3' 2-6-2T No. 82009 departs with a westbound train towards Aberdovey in May 1962. It had arrived at Machynlleth from Bristol St. Philip's Marsh in February 1961.

Left: A schoolboy winds on his camera after photographing BR Standard Class '3' 2-6-2T No. 82034 at Gogarth Halt in 1964. It was at Machynlleth from April 1961 until early 1965 when it left for Patricroft along with the other 2-6-2Ts from that shed, Nos. 82000/3/9/31.

Dovey Junction

Dovey Junction, which was Glandovey Junction until 1904, was where the Cambrian Coast line from Barmouth in the north met the line which came up from Aberystwyth in the south. It was purely an interchange station built on an area of marshland and was never provided with a public road or footpath.

The ground was very soft and therefore all of the buildings were built on piles sixty feet deep; the platforms had to be made from timber. The original station was subject to flooding as the platforms, running lines and sidings at the Machynlleth end sank while the station building which was supported on deep piles stayed firm. Reconstruction plans were produced in 1951 but work did not start until 1955 and was not completed until February 1959, with three lightweight modular buildings and a new signal box, all floating on three-foot deep concrete rafts.

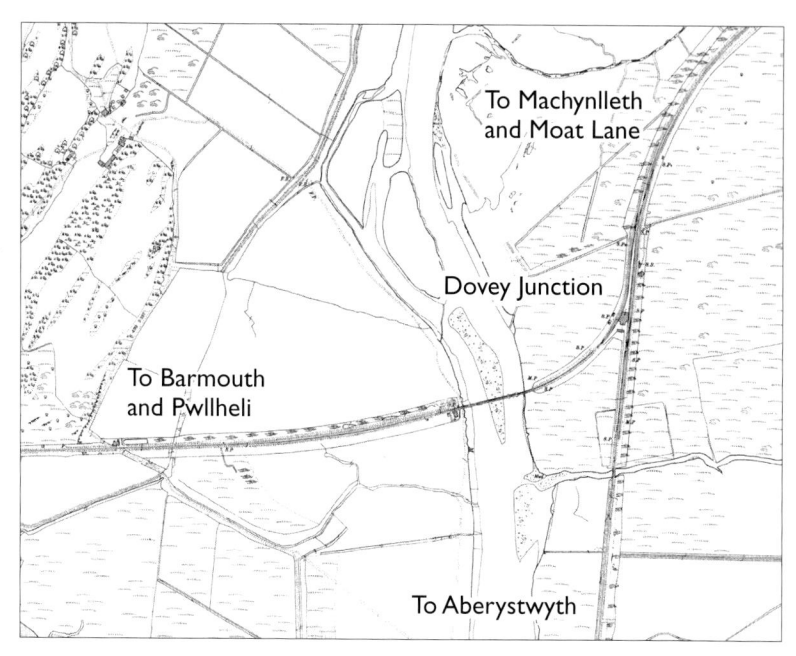

The remoteness of the location is well illustrated in this picture of BR Standard Class '4' 4-6-0 No. 75006 waiting with an eastbound train in 1957. The original 1890 signal box is still in place but the GWR signal on the right with a three-way route indicator had replaced a Cambrian Railways' multi-arm signal. Note the '45XX' 2-6-2T on the rear of the train; it will take the stock back down to the coast while No. 75006 goes to Machynlleth for servicing since there were no watering facilities at Dovey Junction. The Aberystwyth platform on the left could accommodate nine coaches whereas the Barmouth one on the right was much shorter taking only five coaches.

CHAPTER 5 - BARMOUTH JUNCTION TO DOVEY JUNCTION

The two Up 'Cambrian Coast Express' portions stand side-by-side at Dovey Junction, probably in 1958. On the left, Churchward '43XX' 2-6-0 No. 4377 has arrived from Aberystwyth and on the right '90XX' 4-4-0 No. 9013 with the Pwllheli portion. After No. 9013 has been uncoupled, No. 4377 which has already left its coaches, will collect them and add them to its train. In 1958 the 'Cambrian Coast Express' left Aberystwyth at 11.45am, arriving at Paddington at 6.0pm. In the reverse direction, the Down train divided at Machynlleth. The 2-6-0 was built in 1915 and based at Machynlleth from November 1955 until withdrawn in January 1959. The 'Dukedog' was there from 1937 until withdrawn at the end of 1958. Note the old style train headboard on No. 9013 and the later pattern on No. 4377. The Cambrian Railways signalbox is still in place although the wooden station buildings have gone and been replaced with the prefabricated structures.

'90XX' 4-4-0 No. 9000 from Machynlleth shed standing on the loop opposite the coast line platform, facing towards Machynlleth, in a picture post-1952 because the smokebox number plate was not fitted until then; it was withdrawn from Machynlleth in March 1955. No. 9000 has a lined-out tender, presumably from 9009 or 9014, a replacement later pattern boiler with top feed and upper lamp iron fixed to the smokebox door, and large sandboxes. Despite its number, it was the second of the rebuilt engines into service in May 1936 as No. 3200 *Earl of Mount Edgcumbe*, using the number originally intended for 3265; the first engine 3201 taking the following number. The single wagon in the train is a L&NER standard 13-tonner with a broken back, a common weakness of early L&NER-built vehicles.

Collett '2251' 0-6-0 No. 2286 waits in the Barmouth platform at Dovey Junction with a train to Pwllheli in around 1960. It was allocated to Machynlleth from July 1955 until October 1962 when it was transferred to Hereford.

With silver-painted buffers and smokebox door handles and highly polished by the staff at Aberystwyth shed for the 'Cambrian Coast Express', No. 7818 *Granville Manor* is backing the four-coach portion from Pwllheli on to the coaches which it had brought in from Aberystwyth. Note the maroon ex-L&NER Gresley Scottish Region-allocated coach at the front contrasting with the 'chocolate and cream' BR Mark 1 coaches making up the rest of the Paddington-bound train.

Unlike the Great Western running-in boards, their British Railways replacements merely had the station name and not the destinations served. Green-liveried BR Standard Class '3' 2-6-2T No. 82020 waits with a train for the coastal line to Barmouth and Pwllheli.

Ivatt Class '2' 2-6-0 No. 46518 is approaching the station with a seven-coach train to the coast, probably a summer Saturday working to Barmouth and Pwllheli, in the early 1960s. It was built at Swindon in January 1953 and was at Brecon until October 1959 when it moved to Oswestry. The lower trespass sign is of Cambrian Railways origin, its Cambrian Railways heading overpainted, while the one above it is a BR Western Region sign.

BR Standard Class '4' 2-6-4T No. 80097 arriving at Dovey Junction from Aberystwyth, probably in 1964. After it was displaced by electrification on the London, Tilbury & Southend line in July 1962 No. 80097 went briefly to Old Oak Common for storage, then to Swansea (East Dock) and to Oswestry in July 1963 and on to Machynlleth in June 1964. It was rescued from Barry scrapyard in May 1985 and given a complete rebuild by the 'Bury Standard 4 Group' which took thirty-four years before it finally re-entered service in March 2019. The track on the left was the main shunting neck where empty carriages were often parked. This platform was extended beyond the loop points by the Great Western Railway in 1923 so that a short incoming train could arrive, its passengers get on or off, and then cross a Down train in the loop (although previously extended in 1890 it had been dismantled in 1919 with the timber used to repair the other platforms).

Shirt-sleeved Permanent Way workers are busy at the eastern end of the station as the driver of BR Standard Class '4' 2-6-4T No. 80099 watches from his cab. It followed a similar path to Machynlleth after leaving the LT&S in July 1962 as No. 80097, but after withdrawal in May 1965 it was not so fortunate and was scrapped two months later by G.Cohen at Morriston. Note the Permanent Way Department crane mounted on an adapted 'Grampus' ballast wagon, its removable ends allowing easy access from an end loading dock.

CHAPTER 5 - BARMOUTH JUNCTION TO DOVEY JUNCTION

No. 7810 *Draycott Manor* at Dovey Junction with the Up 'Cambrian Coast Express' which it has brought in from Aberystwyth on 24th July 1963. On the right, a BR Standard Class '4' 2-6-4T brings in the portion from Pwllheli that will be added to *Draycott Manor*'s train. No. 7802 was allocated to Oswestry from September 1959 until the end of 1963 when it moved to Machynlleth. The last steam hauled 'Cambrian Coast Express' working between Aberystwyth and Shrewsbury occurred on 4th March 1967, using BR Standard Class '4' 4-6-0 No. 75033 on the Up train, and No. 75021 on the Down working; the service lost its name at the end of the 1967 season. The prefabricated signal box and station buildings on the narrow platform are visible between the two trains. The line from Barmouth crossed over the River Dovey on a bridge just out of picture on the right and dropped down into the platform.

Brian Stephenson

6 – Dovey Junction to Aberystwyth

The line south from Dovey Junction to Aberystwyth was opened by the Aberystwith [sic] & Welsh Coast Railway in two stages, firstly to Borth in July 1863 and then down to Aberystwyth in June 1864. In July 1865 the company was absorbed by the Cambrian Railways which had been formed the previous year.

The route followed the coast as far as Borth, and was mostly level, but from there southbound trains had to climb the 1 in 60/75 of Llandre Bank before descending into Bow Street and then there was another 1 in 75 climb before the line dropped down towards Aberystwyth.

Glandyfi

No. 7823 *Hook Norton Manor* leaves Glandyfi with the Aberystwyth portion of the 'Cambrian Coast Express' as a northbound train waits in the station on 2nd June 1962. Although officially allocated to Machynlleth, the British Railways built 'Manor' would actually have been based at its Aberystwyth sub-shed. Unlike many of its classmates *Hook Norton Manor* was scrapped following withdrawal in July 1964. The first coach in the train is the unique mini-buffet 'Autobar' which was converted in early 1962 from Mark 1 SK No. W25189. One compartment adjoining the centre vestibule was taken out and a group of nine coin-operated vending machines installed. Six machines dispensed snacks, two sold cold bottled soft drinks and one cigarettes. It is just possible to see that the fourth window has been replaced with a sign that read 'auto buffet – snacks soft drinks confectionery cigarettes'. The coach ran only between Shrewsbury and Aberystwyth, always running behind the engine and was turned on the triangle at each end. There was about an hour between the arrival at Shrewsbury of the Up train before the Down train arrived from Paddington, allowing the machines to be inspected and re-stocked. The name of the station was changed in 1904 from Glandovey to Glandyfi to end the confusion with Glandovey Junction which became Dovey Junction at the same date; it closed in June 1965. Note the GWR clerestory Camping Coach on the right.
Ben Brooksbank

Ynyslas

'90XX' 4-4-0 No. 9021 at Ynyslas in the mid-1950s. It was always on the Cambrian until withdrawn in December 1958, although it had been in store from much of 1956 onwards, emerging only for the summer timetable. No. 9021 has a later pattern of boiler with top feed. The Ynyslas station building, hidden behind the signal box, had to have its upper storey removed to prevent it from sinking into the peat bog on which the station was built.

The single line token is about to be exchanged as BR Standard Class '4' 2-6-4T No. 80132 arrives at Ynyslas with the 8.17am Oswestry to Aberystwyth train on 19th August 1963. Originally on the London, Tilbury & Southend from new in 1956 until July 1962 when it moved to Old Oak Common, then Shrewsbury in November and on to Oswestry in January 1963; No. 80132 was transferred to Bangor in January 1965. Another effect of the removal of the upper storey of the station building was the drop in height down to the original platform in the foreground of this picture. Drivers of Down trains were instructed to stop with the coaches at the higher part of the platform if possible. The shelter on the Up platform was small and basic. It had kept the early style of displaying the station name which had long been superseded by running-in boards. At the end of the shelter nearest the camera is the even smaller former signal box which had been replaced by 1896 by the one on the right which has a tarpaulin across the gable end. The latter was closed on 7th September 1963, and the loop taken out shortly afterwards.
M.J. Fox/Rail Archive Stephenson

Borth

The signals are off for '90XX' 4-4-0 No. 9005 to depart from Borth with a three-coach local to Aberystwyth once the crew have finished posing for the cameraman. When rebuilt from 'Duke' No. 3255 and 'Bulldog' No. 3413 in September 1936 as No. 3205 it had the name *Earl of Devon* but this was removed in June 1937. It was renumbered to 9005 in July 1946, transferred from Machynlleth to Oswestry in July 1956 and withdrawn there in July 1959. At the Aberystwyth end of the station there was a public footpath crossing (immediately in front of the train) as well as a railway barrow crossing. The signal is a nice early GWR square post type erected after the 1923 Grouping.

A BR Standard Class '4' 2-6-4T waits at Borth with an early morning train to Machynlleth, probably in 1964. There are still two pints of milk on the Camping Coach stepboard as the lady on the platform chats to one of the occupants. In 1957 the Western Region also had 8-berth coaches at many other locations including Aberdovey, Barmouth Junction, Carrog, Duffryn Ardudwy, Fairbourne, Llwyngwril and Talsarnau. There had been a Camping Coach at Borth since 1934.

Another Standard Class '4' 2-6-4T, No. 80136, which has piloted a LM&SR Ivatt Class '2' 2-6-0 over the 1 in 60/75 of Llandre Bank on a train to Aberystwyth. After six years on the LT&S it moved to Shrewsbury in July 1962, staying until January 1963 when it went to Oswestry, then on to Machynlleth in June 1964 ending its days at Shrewsbury from September 1964. After withdrawal in July 1965 it languished at Barry scrapyard until 1979 when it was purchased privately and slowly restored to working order, steaming again in 1998. No. 80136 is currently operating on the North Yorkshire Moors Railway having completed a full overhaul in 2016. The small water tank on the right was mainly used to replenish the tanks on assisting engines before they returned back to Aberystwyth.

On a bright sunlit day showing the Cambrian scenery at its best, BR Standard Class '4' 2-6-4T No. 80132 arrives at Borth from Aberystwyth in 1964. One of the former London, Tilbury & Southend engines, it arrived on the Cambrian at Oswestry in January 1963 before going to Bangor in January 1965.

The last of the Great Western pre-war built 'Manor' 4-6-0s No. 7819 *Hinton Manor* with the Up 'Cambrian Coast Express' at Borth on 19th August 1963. After withdrawal No. 7819 was purchased from Woodham Brothers at Barry in 1973 and worked on the Severn Valley Railway from 1977 after being restored there, and also on the main line including visits to Aberystwyth and Pwllheli in summer 1987 working the 'Cardigan Bay Express'. It is now owned by the SVR Charitable Trust and is on static display at The Engine House, Highley. The first coach in the train, contrasting with the maroon coaches behind, is the 'chocolate and cream' liveried mini-buffet 'Autobar' which ran on the 'Cambrian Coast Express' between Shrewsbury and Aberystwyth from early 1962. It was always positioned behind the engine and was turned on the triangles at each end of the journey.

M.J. Fox/Rail Archive Stephenson

Aberystwyth

From August 1867 the Cambrian's rather basic station facilities at Aberystwyth were shared by the Manchester & Milford Railway's line from Strata Florida and Pencader which reached Carmarthen over the Carmarthen and Cardigan Railway. Over the next two decades the station was gradually improved and by 1888 the Manchester & Milford had its own platforms on the southern side of the Cambrian's arrival platforms. The company had been beset by financial difficulties from the outset and eventually in 1906 was leased by the Great Western Railway which took it over in 1911; joint working of the station between the Great Western Railway and Cambrian Railways came into effect in March 1908.

Both companies wanted to improve the station facilities to cope with the level of traffic which had developed but they were thwarted by the local town council which refused to sell the land needed. After the end of the First World War the council relented but the Cambrian Railways' poor financial position meant that it was not until after the 1923 Grouping that redevelopment finally started. In the event all the works were squeezed into land already owned by the GWR. A new station building was built in a neo-Georgian style and the platforms extended and provided with canopies. Additional sidings were put in for carriage cleaning, the engine shed was improved, and the Vale of Rheidol line was extended from its original passenger terminus to a new site alongside the main line station.

The Carmarthen to Aberystwyth line was closed in December 1964, and in May 1968 the Vale of Rheidol line station was moved into what had been Platforms 4 and 5 of the standard gauge station, the former Manchester & Milford Railway Carmarthen bays.

This 1965 map shows the layout of the main line and narrow gauge lines at Aberystwyth as they co-existed between 1926 and 1968.

Approaches

No. 7802 *Bradley Manor* departing from Aberystwyth on 12th April 1950 No. 7802 was allocated to the Aberystwyth sub-shed of Machynlleth for over fifteen years, from 1946 until 1962. It was probably working a daily turn between Aberystwyth and Shrewsbury which left Aberystwyth at 10.0am, arrived at Shrewsbury at 1.28pm, and returned with the 3.10pm from Shrewsbury which arrived back at 6.0pm. On the right of the picture is the Plas Crug tower which was said to be the remains of a 17th century manor house on the site of Castle Rheidol; it was demolished in 1967.

'Manor' 4-6-0 No. 7822 *Foxcote Manor* from Oswestry shed shortly after departing from Aberystwyth with the 6.0pm train to Shrewsbury on 5th April 1962. It was preserved by the 'Foxcote Manor Society' who bought it in 1972 from Woodhams' scrapyard at Barry and has been based on the Llangollen Railway since 1985. *D.M.C. Hepburne-Scott/Rail Archive Stephenson*

Ivatt Class '2' 2-6-0 No. 46515 heads away from Aberystwyth with an evening train to Machynlleth on 5th April 1964. When built at Swindon in January 1953 it was allocated to Oswestry and remained there until the shed closed in January 1965, when it moved to Speke Junction. No. 46515 was repainted in lined green with a small BR crest during an overhaul at Caerphilly in January 1960. *D.M.C. Hepburne-Scott/Rail Archive Stephenson*

BR Standard Class '4' 2-6-4T No. 80104 heads away from Aberystwyth with a goods train for Machynlleth consisting mostly of vans, a container, a 'Fruit D' van and returning oil empties, on 6th April 1964. Originally a London, Tilbury & Southend line engine it went to Croes Newydd in November 1962 and its final allocation was at Machynlleth in March 1963 where it stayed until withdrawn in July 1965. No. 80104 was preserved on the Swanage Railway after purchase from Barry scrapyard by the Southern Steam Trust in 1984. It was cosmetically restored and was bought by a group of supporters in 1988. After it was returned to working order in 1997 it has operated on the Swanage Railway ever since. *D.M.C. Hepburne-Scott/Rail Archive Stephenson*

Station

The new station constructed by the Great Western Railway between 1923 and 1925 was built in neo-Georgian style, clad in Portland stone, with an impressive four-sided clock tower visible from all over the town and which is in the centre right background of this picture. The platforms were extended and provided with standard GWR pattern canopies. They were numbered from left to right 5 to 1. The Vale of Rheidol station which was relocated as part of the work in 1925 is on the far left behind the wall of Platform 5 which was used by Carmarthen line trains. In the distance in Platform 2 is No. 7828 *Odney Manor* on a local service. It was the penultimate BR-built 'Manor' and was rescued from Barry Docks for preservation in 1981 and has worked on the West Somerset Railway since the early 1990s. On the right is the small goods yard and the goods shed built in 1933.

The frames of withdrawn 'Bulldog' 4-4-0 No. 3411 *Stanley Baldwin* were used with the boiler and cab of condemned 'Duke' 4-4-0 No. 3259 *Merlin* to produce '90XX' 4-4-0 No. 3221 in November 1938. Renumbered to 9021 in September 1946, it has steam to spare as it waits to depart from Aberystwyth in the early 1950s. No. 9021 was always on the Cambrian, at Aberystwyth until withdrawn in December 1958, although it was in store from much of 1956 onwards, emerging only for the summer timetable. No. 9021 has a later pattern of boiler with top feed but reverted to the earlier type in April 1958. Unusually, unlike on the other platforms, the starting signal on Platform 2 is positioned part-way down the platform, immediately outside the extended canopies that were added under the GWR modernisation in the mid-1920s.

No. 7811 *Dunley Manor* departs from Aberystwyth with the 'Cambrian Coast Express' to Paddington past the former Cambrian Aberystwyth Signal Box on 29th July 1959. The mid-1950s saw the new British Railways Mark I coaches in use on the principal expresses, with 'chocolate and cream' sets employed on the 'Cambrian Coast Express' from 1957. The signal box was closed in April 1982.
R.O. Tuck/Rail Archive Stephenson

The first of the class, entering service in February 1938, No. 7800 *Torquay Manor* waits to depart from Aberystwyth with the 6.0pm to Shrewsbury on 22nd June 1962. The 'Manor' was essentially a lighter version of the 'Grange' 4-6-0, both classes introduced as replacements for withdrawn '43XX' 2-6-0s. Although the Cambrian main line from Whitchurch to Aberystwyth was classified by the GWR as a 'yellow' route, certain 'blue' category engines including the 'Manor' 4-6-0s were permitted from 1943 onwards. Following the GWR tradition of naming engines in alphabetical order No. 7800 was allocated the name *Anthony Manor* but instead received the name *Torquay Manor*.

Aberystwyth was a long way from Ivatt Class '2' 2-6-0 No. 46518's home shed of Oswestry. The class was less common this far west than the BR Standard 2-6-0s. However, this changed near the end of steam on the Cambrian after the closure of the Mid-Wales line and the Hereford-Three Cocks-Brecon line in 1962 took away many of their duties. No. 46518 moved to Speke Junction in January 1965 when Oswestry shed closed. Note the full load of Fyffes bananas being delivered to the goods shed on the right.

When the BR Standard Class '4' 2-6-4Ts arrived on the Cambrian in 1962 they were employed on the same passenger work as the tender engines. No. 80099 was preparing to work the 6.20pm to York from Aberystwyth's Platform 1 in 1964. It was at Machynlleth from July 1963 until withdrawal in May 1965.

CHAPTER 6 - DOVEY JUNCTION TO ABERYSTWYTH 115

With the engine shed in the background, BR Standard Class '3' 2-6-2T No. 82000 at Aberystwyth in 1964 is shunting fuel tanks, a staple revenue source for the Cambrian Coast line until the late 1970s. It was at Machynlleth from January 1960 until March 1965 when it went to the London Midland Region at Patricroft for its last two years in service. The 2-6-2Ts had taken over the Aberystwyth pilot duties from GWR '54XX' and '74XX' Pannier tanks.

The canopies have been cut back in this view of BR Sulzer Class '24' diesel-electric No. 5084 at Aberystwyth on 10th June 1971. To the left is a blue-liveried Vale of Rheidol open summer car in the headshunt, alongside the ramp giving access to the Vale of Rheidol ground level platform. No. 5084 was built at Crewe in April 1960 for the Eastern Region but was immediately loaned to the London Midland Region at Rugby. It moved to Cricklewood at the end of the year and stayed in the London area until April 1967 when it was transferred to the Stoke Division (D05). It has shortened fuel and water tanks and is in blue livery with full yellow ends and BR double arrow emblems, but still has its pre-TOPS number and bodyside hand and footholds.

Shed

'90XX' 4-4-0 No. 9000 in unlined BR black livery on 16th April 1952 has a replacement later pattern boiler with top feed and the upper lamp iron fixed to the smokebox door, and large sandboxes. Despite its number, it was the second of the rebuilt engines into service in May 1936 as No. 3200 *Earl of Mount Edgcumbe*, using the number originally intended for 3265; the first engine No. 3201 which entered traffic in April 1936 took the following number. No. 9000 was included in the 1954 Locomotive Condemnation Programme and was withdrawn in March 1955. Note in the background an elderly GWR square wooden post Home signal with a route indicator giving the choice of four routes, probably Platforms 5 to 2.

'2251' 0-6-0 No. 2200 at the 'country' end of Aberystwyth shed on 23rd June 1956. The stationary boiler on the left was removed by 1961. Although the lowest numbered engine in the class it was not built until June 1938, eight years after No. 2251 entered service. The shed in the background was built in 1938, replacing an earlier Cambrian Railways shed. In May 1968 it became the home of the Vale of Rheidol locomotives and stock.

CHAPTER 6 - DOVEY JUNCTION TO ABERYSTWYTH

The cleaning gang pose on an immaculate No. 7802 *Bradley Manor* polished to perfection for the 'Cambrian Coast Express' on 15th May 1959. Mr. Rowlands, Aberystwyth's shedmaster, kept the engines for this train in showroom condition, even having silver-painted buffer heads and smokebox door fittings! The Western Region re-introduced 'chocolate and cream' livery for its named expresses in 1956 and both headboards and coach boards were in GWR-style Roman lettering. The plain aluminium on black headboard introduced in 1953 was replaced in summer 1957 by the crested pattern with black lettering on a cream background incorporating the Cambrian Railways coat-of-arms (with a green Welsh Dragon on the left and a red English demi-rose on the right) and these were in use until the final steam-hauled run on 4th March 1967, the last WR headboard in service. No. 7800 *Torquay Manor* in the background is in less immaculate condition. Note the signal has been updated with a tubular post replacement, still with a route indicator. The engine stands on the site of the present day Vale of Rheidol Railway engineering works which was opened in 2012.

Two 'Manors' in front of the shed on 29th July 1961 are in more workaday condition than No. 7802 above; on the left No. 7814 *Fringford Manor* which was on Machynlleth's books but effectively at Aberystwyth from February 1959 until January 1963, and on the right No. 7816 *Frilsham Manor* from Tyseley where it was allocated between October 1960 and October 1961. Neither was preserved.

7 – Vale of Rheidol Light Railway

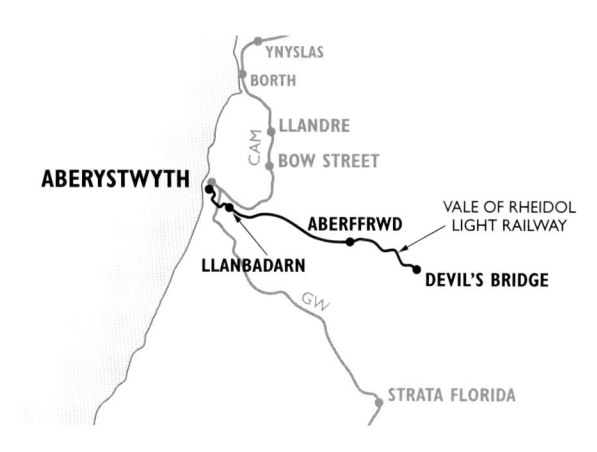

1960 Western Region timetable leaflet.

Although the Manchester & Milford Railway had obtained powers in 1861 to construct a branch from its proposed main line at Devil's Bridge through the Rheidol Valley to Aberystwyth, it was not until 1897 that the Vale of Rheidol (Light) Railway Act was passed. By this date Devil's Bridge had become a well-known tourist attraction and the lead mining industry was developing in the Rheidol Valley, and the new railway looked to tap into both markets. The 11¾ miles long 1ft 11½in. gauge line between Aberystwyth and Devil's Bridge was opened to goods in August 1902 although regular passenger services did not begin until December 1902. After a dispute between one of the company's shareholders, the contractor who had taken shares as part of the payment for construction work, his shares were purchased by Cambrian Railways and it subsequently acquired the whole company in 1913.

Stations were provided initially at Aberystwyth, Llanbadarn, Capel Bangor, Nantyronen, Aberffrwd, and Devil's Bridge. The route out of Aberystwyth had to weave around the standard gauge tracks, the Vale of Rheidol line resembling a large 'U' shape with the River Rheidol at its base. It passed beneath the north end of the Manchester & Milford Railway river bridge, before turning sharply to run parallel alongside the Cambrian Railways approach tracks as far as the station at Llanbadarn. The line climbed from 14ft above sea level at the coast to 680ft at Devil's Bridge, in three stages. The first five miles from Aberystwyth ran along the floor of the Afon Rheidol Valley, with mainly level stretches punctuated by gentle rises of 1 in 264 and 1 in 132. At Capel Bangor the line was still only around 100ft above sea level but for the next 2½ miles to Aberffrwd it climbed the valley side with some level sections punctuating stretches at 1 in 50. The final 4¼ miles from 280ft above sea level through the steep wooded southern slope of Cwm Rheidol was a continuous unrelieved 1 in 50.

Motive power was provided by two outside-framed 2-6-2Ts, No. 1 *Edward VII* and No. 2 *Prince of Wales*, purchased from the Manchester firm Davies & Metcalfe Ltd. and a small 2-4-0T, No. 3 *Rheidol*, built by Bagnall of Stafford which was acquired from the contractor in 1903. When the Cambrian took control in 1913 there were twelve 32ft bogie coaches, three four-wheel guards vans, two four-wheel open coaches and a variety of goods stock, including side-door, end-door and flat wagons. The Great Western Railway built two new 2-6-2Ts (Nos. 7 and 8) at Swindon in July 1923 and withdrew the 2-4-0T in 1924. Davies & Metcalfe No. 1 (1212) remained as a spare engine, ending its days at Swindon in 1932. No. 2 (1213) was sent to Swindon for overhaul in 1923, but was scrapped and replaced by a brand new engine with the same number in 1924.

A new station at Aberystwyth was opened in 1926 alongside the main line station. The GWR continued to invest in the line, building new carriages in 1938 to replace the earlier stock; these are still in use today. In January 1931 the year-round passenger service ended, becoming summer only and the goods service was withdrawn. Operations were suspended during the Second World War and passenger numbers were slow to recover and closure was seriously considered at the end of 1954. Fortunately, before the 1955 season, British Railways began a publicity drive extolling the spectacular scenery of the valley and introduced cheap evening excursions, and passenger numbers increased dramatically. In 1956 the three engines were named and for the 1957 season they were repainted into fully lined-out green passenger livery, with matching 'chocolate and cream' coaches.

Following the closure of the Carmarthen to Aberystwyth line, the station in Aberystwyth was moved the short distance into what had been Platforms 4 and 5 of the standard gauge station, and from May 1968 trains used a new line which ran between the former standard gauge engine shed and its water tower. This allowed the old route and its 'flagged' level crossing at Park Avenue to be abandoned. At the same time the old shed near the river was closed and the narrow gauge locomotives and stock used the standard gauge shed. In 1989 the Vale of Rheidol became the first part of British Rail to be privatised when it was sold to the Brecon Mountain Railway, which in a pre-arranged deal then sold it on to the Phyllis Rampton Narrow Gauge Railway Trust in 1996. The line is now marketed under the 'Great Little Trains of Wales' banner. In 2012 a brand-new fully equipped workshop was opened and in June 2019 a new 1930s-style station with a GWR 'pagoda' pattern lavatory building was opened as part of ongoing development of the site at Aberystwyth.

Aberystwyth

Not yet named and painted in unlined green with British Railways' emblems on the tank sides, Nos. 7 and 8 prepare for departure from Aberystwyth on 3rd August 1955. The second vehicle in the train is a 'summer' coach, with open upper sides but equipped with weather curtains which have been rolled away on this sunny summer's day. The carriages are in crimson lake and cream livery. The building on the right is the rehearsal room of the Aberystwyth Silver Band. The canopies of the main line station are visible above the train. *Rail Archive Stephenson*

No. 7 *Owain Glyndŵr* on 29th July 1961 outside the original 1902 engine shed which was located near the river. The water tank was built by the GWR in 1924 from old Cambrian cast iron panels and was fed from the large water tank at the Aberystwyth standard gauge shed. To the left of the water tank is the trackbed of the former harbour branch which fell into disuse around 1930, and beyond is the harbour itself. The line into the station ran to the right of the shed. The side-door coal wagon was built in 1906 by the Midland Railway Carriage & Wagon Co., Shrewsbury. In 1968 after the line was diverted to the Carmarthen platforms of the main station, the standard gauge steam shed was converted for narrow gauge use and the shed in this picture was demolished. Crews for the line were provided from the main line shed, generally with the older drivers, working turn and turn about from their normal work. It must have been a pleasant change for them to work the little engines in the summer months, although the cabs would have been considerably warmer! Coal for the engines was brought from the 'broad gauge' shed to an exchange siding where the Vale of Rheidol shedman would unload it into trucks which had to be worked round to the narrow gauge shed. The coal was carefully chosen for quality and obtained from the Ogilvie Colliery in South Wales (closed in 1975) as far as possible, and even then, was checked for impurities such as pyrite (iron sulphide) before it was loaded into the engine bunkers. Under the London Midland Region, coal was brought in from Maltby which never performed quite like Welsh steam coal.

A bus conductor from the Crosville garage (out of picture to the left) carries on with his chat as No. 7 *Owain Glyndŵr* eases past the neighbouring house and crosses the level crossing over Park Avenue as it backs down to Aberystwyth terminus, having coaled and watered at the shed on 29th July 1961. To ensure that sufficient coal was carried, the bunkers were filled to overflowing, and prime lumps would be stacked on the footplate. From 1926 until the 1968 season all Vale of Rheidol trains had to be flagged across Park Avenue and the flagman's arm just protrudes into the extreme right of this photograph. The original Vale of Rheidol 1902 terminus was located near the parked car in the distance. In 1926 the GWR extended the line across Smithfield Road (later Park Avenue) to a new station alongside the mainline terminus. The land thus released was sold and the Crosville bus garage was built. The row of modern terraced houses behind the engine were also built on land formerly occupied by the Vale of Rheidol terminus. Above the fence at the left of the picture are several Vale of Rheidol carriages standing in the carriage siding; until 1968 most of them were stored in the open. At the same date, the line was re-routed to run into the former Carmarthen line platforms in the main line station, eliminating this level crossing and the 'dog-leg' route to the southern side of the station. Note the standard GWR trespass sign, and also the absence of litter.

CHAPTER 7 - VALE OF RHEIDOL LIGHT RAILWAY

No. 7 *Owain Glyndŵr* waits at the 1926 terminus on 29th July 1961. Beyond is the main line station with the canopies added by the GWR during its rebuild from 1924 to 1926. In 1968 the Vale of Rheidol trains were relocated into the main line station where these canopies dwarfed the narrow gauge trains. It is intriguing to speculate why the locals would want to buy their suits from a Hepworths' caravan in a railway station car park!

A view of No. 7 *Owain Glyndŵr* from the other direction as it waits for the starting signal to be pulled off for departure to Devil's Bridge on 29th July 1961. The small Vale of Rheidol signal cabin, the only signal cabin on the line, is alongside the level crossing just ahead of the engine. The large building in the distance is the Crosville bus garage. Note the 5mph limit sign, to the left of the Dutton signal which has lost its finial.

No. 9 *Prince of Wales* returns home from Swindon following an overhaul on 20th April 1960. The train includes the Shrewsbury breakdown crane which would lift No. 9 back onto the narrow gauge rails at the Vale of Rheidol transfer siding just outside Aberystwyth station. No. 7 *Owain Glyndŵr* waits to haul No. 9 back to the Vale of Rheidol shed. Note the diminutive Vale of Rheidol wagons in new BR light grey paint, loaded with fresh ballast.

In May 1968 the Vale of Rheidol station was relocated from its 1926 GWR terminus to the main line station at Aberystwyth. Corporate blue-liveried No. 7 *Owain Glyndŵr* waits to depart with a well patronised six-coach train for Devil's Bridge in 1973. The platforms were formerly used by the Carmarthen line trains which had ceased at the end of 1964. The standard gauge bay platforms were too high for the narrow gauge trains so a track level island platform was accessed via a ramp between the buffer stops. The platform canopies of 1925 were cut back in 1971, leaving a small section behind the buffer stops and revealing the original Cambrian Railways' gothic awnings attached to the surviving Cambrian building. The clock tower of the GWR's new 1925 neo-Georgian station building overlooks the scene. The former Manchester & Milford bay is now occupied by a new Vale of Rheidol carriage shed. The engine's tank is fitted with electric lighting cable for use with the 'Night Rheidol' trains introduced in the early 1970s and it no longer has a smokebox number plate. The boilers on the narrow gauge engines were maintained to the highest standards by British Rail and set the standard for steam boiler maintenance following the end of steam on the main line.

Derek Lowe Archive

Llanbadarn

With Aberystwyth gas works in the background, No. 7 *Owain Glyndŵr* waits at Llanbadarn with a train to Devil's Bridge on 28th August 1959. The carriages are painted in Western Region 'chocolate and cream' and the engine is lined green with a British Railways' emblem on the tanks. Note the guard on the carriage footboards. As part of its investment in the line between the wars, the Great Western replaced the original nine closed coaches with an equivalent number of new vehicles in time for the 1938 season. There were seven all-Third carriages, later Second class, and two brake Thirds which were included to avoid the need for a separate four-wheel brake van. These used reconditioned bogies from the coaches they replaced, allowing the GWR to treat them as rebuilds for tax purposes! They had steel-panelled flush-sided bodies and were mounted on new steel underframes. There were no internal partitions, allowing an unobstructed view of the scenery and there was no heating or lighting in view of the operation of summer-only services, possibly a trifle optimistically given the vagaries of British summer weather!
Rail Archive Stephenson

No. 8 *Llywelyn* pulls into Llanbadarn on its way back to Aberystwyth, which was less than a mile away, on 24th July 1963. No. 8 had been built at Swindon together with No. 7 in 1923, as replacements for the original Vale of Rheidol 2-4-0T and the two 2-6-2Ts built by Davies & Metcalfe in 1902.

Aberffrwd

No. 8 *Llywelyn* arrives at Aberffrwd with a Devil's Bridge train on 22nd July 1969. This was the main intermediate station on the line, 280ft above sea level with another 400ft still to climb on the final four miles to Devil's Bridge. British Railways' removal of the passing loops at Capel Bangor and Aberffrwd had created a railway on which trains could no longer pass between Aberystwyth and Devil's Bridge. This significantly changed the operation of the railway – up to three trains would head up the line in succession, all waiting at Devil's Bridge together before each returned down to the coast. Note the British Rail corporate rail alphabet running-in board showing an incorrect elevation. On the left is the 2,500 gallon cast iron water tank erected by the Cambrian Railways in 1919. By the time of this photograph, the Vale of Rheidol engines were the last remaining steam locomotives operating on British Rail. The new rail blue corporate livery with white double arrows was applied to the locomotives and carriages in time for the 1968 season. The 1950s Gill Sans smokebox door number plates lasted until the early 1970s, when yellow-painted GWR-style buffer beam numbers were applied.

Climbing to Devil's Bridge

The scenery in the Rheidol Valley is spectacular and here, near Rhiwfron, the train hauled by No. 9 *Prince of Wales* is dwarfed as it climbs the wooded southern slope of Cwm Rheidol on 29th May 1961. The gradient for the final 4¼ miles was 1 in 50 all the way up to Devil's Bridge. On the opposite side of the valley is the ochre-coloured waste from the former lead mining activity which was one of the main reasons for the building of the railway when it was authorised in 1897. However, mine closures rendered traffic from this source almost non-existent by the time the Great Western took over the Cambrian in 1922. The general passenger service ceased at the beginning of 1931 and therafter became summer-only while residual goods traffic ceased in January 1931 because tourism had become the sole reason for the line continuing to exist.

CHAPTER 7 - VALE OF RHEIDOL LIGHT RAILWAY

The section of line between Aberffrwd and Devil's Bridge has a gradient of 1 in 50 and numerous sharp, check-railed curves on the steep wooded southern slopes of Cwm Rheidol. On 24th July 1963, No. 8 *Llywelyn* makes its way up the gradient near Rhiwfron. Although there was only a small halt there, it was originally an important loading place for the products of the Cwm Rheidol mines. A mill processed the extracted ore to remove the waste rock before it was carried on an aerial ropeway to the railway on the opposite side of the valley. The circumstances of this photograph are not recorded, but it was not usual for a crew member to ride on the front footplate. The train is probably stationary while the blower is on to raise steam for the final climb up to Devil's Bridge. The Vale of Rheidol tanks are powerful, sure-footed and free-steaming machines but occasionally wet rails combined with heavy loads would cause slipping and hand sanding 'Darjeeling style' from the front of the engine might be required. The lowered weather curtain on the open carriage would suggest a rainy day.

Having climbed almost 700ft from Aberystwyth No. 7 *Owain Glyndŵr* approaches Devil's Bridge with the 10.0am from Aberystwyth on 27th August 1959. The low building behind the train had formerly been used as a barracks for the contractor's men during construction of the line. The track disappears to the right into quarry cutting. Passengers appear to have opted for the open carriage on this hot summer day. *Rail Archive Stephenson*

No. 7 *Owain Glyndŵr* heads back to Aberystwyth from Devil's Bridge on 24th July 1963. The sharp curves of the narrow gauge line are apparent in this view, and many of them were fitted with check rails. The return journey is all downhill with the locomotive bunker-first. The train is leaving Cwmdauddwr embankment, about to enter Cwmdauddwr cutting as it approaches Aberffrwd.

Devil's Bridge
Devil's Bridge is famous for its three stacked bridges over the Mynach River and the waterfalls where the Mynach drops down around three hundred feet to meet the River Rheidol. In Welsh, it is known as Pontarfynach – 'The bridge over the Mynach river'. The uppermost span was constructed in 1901 over another stone bridge built in 1753 and the original bridge of uncertain date, possibly medieval. According to legend, the lowest bridge was built by the Devil himself to let a local woman rescue her cow which had somehow become stranded on the other side of the gorge. Expecting the woman to walk across to bring it back, the man, dressed in a monk's cowl, had one condition that he would receive the soul of the first living creature to cross the bridge. However, he was tricked by the lady who made her pet dog to run across first – thus leaving the Devil with the soul of a dog! More conventional wisdom says that it is actually an 11th century bridge built by the monks of Strata Florida.

A classic view of Devil's Bridge taken from the footbridge over the rock cutting at the station throat of the terminus on 27th August 1959. The train on the left hauled by No. 7 *Owain Glyndŵr*, which has just arrived, will return as the 5.50pm to Aberystwyth; on the right the 4.0pm departure is headed by No. 9 *Prince of Wales*. In the 1959 Summer Timetable all trains in both directions were scheduled to take exactly one hour for the journey.

The layout and facilities at Devil's Bridge hardly changed over the years. The two passenger tracks to the right of the station building were connected, thereby providing a run-round. There was a stabling siding on one side of the goods shed and two sidings on the other side of the building; the corrugated iron goods shed, built in 1902, was demolished by 1960. The sidings were little used, although before and during the First World War they handled an extensive timber traffic. The starting signal is by Pease/Dutton, operated by the ground frame on the lower right of the picture. In the early days of the railway the station gardens had been planted with rhododendrons which eventually took over the embankment to the right.

The siding contains a spare coach and a four-wheeled brake van. During 1938 the GWR built three of these to replace the Vale of Rheidol originals, re-using some parts of their running gear. They did not have projecting guard's lookouts but had two large windows in the end panel instead. On each side there was a single door with a drop window for the guard and double doors giving access to a spacious luggage compartment. One of the 4-wheel brake vans survives today on the Vale of Rheidol, another is on the Welsh Highland Heritage Railway. *Rail Archive Stephenson*

There is a distinct lack of tourists at Devil's Bridge in the height of the summer as No. 7 *Owain Glyndŵr* gets ready for the return to Aberystwyth on 29th July 1961. The closed carriages had been built new at Swindon in 1938, as replacements for the line's original 1902 match-boarded carriages. Note also the two open summer cars, one with its canvas weather curtains pulled down. In the background is the Vale of Rheidol's only stone-built building, the weighbridge office built in 1905. This building was relocated in 2018 to make way for longer trains and now serves as an information centre for the Vincent Wildlife Trust's Pine Marten Recovery Project and nature trail. The corrugated iron station building dates from 1902 and today is the last surviving original Vale of Rheidol structure; it was given Grade II listing in 1989. The platforms are at ground level, whereas today they have been raised to allow easier and safer access to the carriages. On the left of the photograph, behind the pile of sleepers, is the weedkilling apparatus comprising galvanised tank, sprinkler bar, rubber hoses and cast iron hand water pump which, mounted on a flat manrider trolley, was used by the track gang to spray the ballast with weedkiller. Vale of Rheidol historian C.C. Green complained that it was responsible for killing all the luscious wild strawberries.

The passengers leave their seven-coach train at Devil's Bridge in around 1966 and the driver of No. 9 *Prince of Wales* has left the hot footplate and chats to his mate. No. 9 is still in lined green but the familiar chocolate and cream carriage livery had been discontinued following the control of the Vale of Rheidol moving from Western Region to London Midland Region in 1963. The coaches are in all-over London Midland bronze green with gold 'V OF R' branding. The coaches carried green livery until 1968 when BR rail blue was applied. 'Chocolate and cream' livery eventually made a welcome return in 1983. From the early 1950s Vale of Rheidol locomotives were given 89C Aberystwyth shed plates, a sub-shed of Machynlleth. With the transfer of Machynlleth and the Vale of Rheidol to the London Midland Region in 1963, the code changed to 6F, as carried by No. 9 in this view.

CHAPTER 7 - VALE OF RHEIDOL LIGHT RAILWAY

No. 9 *Prince of Wales* resplendent in the British Railways express lined green livery at Devil's Bridge on 23rd June 1961. It was built in 1924 using the spare boiler made in 1923 when the other two engines, Nos. 7 and 8, were built at Swindon. It was classed as a 'rebuild', presumably for tax purposes, of the original 1902 Davies & Metcalfe engine No. 1213 which was scrapped, and although numbered 1213 it was a completely new engine to exactly the same 1923 design as Nos. 7 and 8. The new No. 1213 was renumbered as No. 9 in March 1949 and repainted at Swindon in plain black. The two rivets either side of the number 9 plate are witness to the earlier and wider 1213 number plate. The steel plate across the cab doorway was to keep coal from spilling off the footplate. The flat bottom rails are held down with spikes in much the same way as they were after the GWR relaid the track in the early/mid 1920s.

The carriage has been repainted in British Railways' crimson lake and cream but No. 7 is still in Great Western livery in this picture at Devil's Bridge in August 1953. It was finally repainted in 1955 in plain green with BR 'lion-over-wheel' emblems, when it also acquired a smokebox number plate.
Robert Darlaston

A young tourist admires No. 8 *Llywelyn* at Devil's Bridge in 1972. The engine and coaches were all in matching rail blue with double arrow symbols for the summer 1968 season. No. 8 has retained the copper-capped chimney, but the backing of the brass name and number plates was changed to plain red from lined black. In 1983 six of the coaches were restored to 'chocolate and cream' livery.

8 – Dovey Junction to Moat Lane Junction

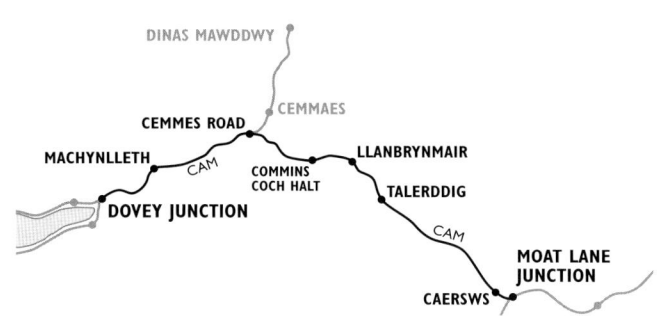

The line east of Dovey Junction to Machynlleth was opened by the Aberystwith & Welsh Coast Railway in 1863 as the first part of its route to Aberystwyth. At Machynlleth it met the Newtown and Machynlleth Railway which had also opened in 1863. The Newtown and Machynlleth Railway diverged at Moat Lane Junction, near to the village of Caersws, from the Llanidloes and Newtown Railway which had opened four years earlier and which met the Mid-Wales Railway line from Three Cocks Junction at Llanidloes.

Machynlleth

This panoramic view of Machynlleth was taken from the cliff behind the engine shed and shows BR Standard Class '4' 4-6-0 No. 75002 arriving with a Pwllheli-Paddington train on 20th August 1966. The large and elaborate station building was constructed from stone excavated from Talerddig cutting and owed its size and style to the Newtown & Machynlleth Company's Chairman Earl Vane who apparently ordered the architect to make his home station the 'best' on the line, delaying its building by almost six months as he added to the specification; it is still in use today. Opposite, and in complete contrast to the building on the Down side, was the small wooden waiting shelter and there was also a GWR 'pagoda' hut immediately to the right of the footbridge. The hut next to the footbridge where the Austin A40 is parked was for the yard foreman and the light-coloured building to the left was the Permanent Way Department salt and weed-killer store. The large dark coloured timber building was the PW Department office, which was moved from Aberdovey in 1925. There is a carpenters' shop behind it and to the right is the PW Sub-Inspector's office. The three large buildings in the centre of the picture were warehouses leased to British Oil & Cake Mills, the animal feed company. Beyond, further to the left, are the cattle pens, which do not appear to have been used for some time, and the Esso petrol unloading facility. The 16-ton mineral wagon loaded with coal is at the end of the shed's turntable road; the shed is off picture to the right.

The second Churchward '45XX' 2-6-2T No. 4501 with an eastbound local train waits at the Up platform on 3rd August 1951. It was built at Wolverhampton Works in November 1906 as GWR No. 2162 and was renumbered in December 1912. No. 4501 was allocated to Machynlleth from April 1941 until it was withdrawn in March 1953. The small waiting shelter on the right was built by the Great Western in 1937 to replace an even smaller Cambrian building. It was perched on an embankment with the foundations reaching back down the slope.

CHAPTER 8 - DOVEY JUNCTION TO MOAT LANE JUNCTION

'4575' class 2-6-2T No. 5570 waits to depart from Machynlleth with the Pwllheli portion of the Down 'Cambrian Coast Express' on 3rd September 1956. This was one of the rare instances where a tank engine regularly carried a named train headboard. The Down train divided into Aberystwyth and Pwllheli portions at Machynlleth, but the Up train combined them at Dovey Junction. No. 5570 was allocated to Machynlleth from 1936 until February 1960 when it moved to Penzance. This picture shows how the two platforms were offset and also the small 13-lever West signal box on the Down platform that was closed when the new signal box was opened in 1959.
C.R.L. Coles/Rail Archive Stephenson

BR Standard Class '2' 2-6-0 No. 78002 assists BR Standard Class '4' 4-6-0 No. 75006 at Machynlleth on the Up 'Cambrian Coast Express' in the mid-1950s. No. 75006 was allocated to Oswestry from December 1953 to August 1958 when the shed's Standard Class '4' 4-6-0s, Nos. 75005/6/20/6/8, moved to Chester West in exchange for its remaining 'Manor' 4-6-0s after responsibility for Chester West depot was transferred from the Western Region to the London Midland Region. No. 78002 was at Machynlleth from May 1953 until September 1963 when it moved to Wigan Central. Note towards the back of the train the change in gradient down from the level section in the middle of the 'hump' through the station.

This picture dating from around 1957 looking east from the footbridge towards Cemmes Road has lots of interesting detail. It was taken before the new goods shed was built in 1960 and the original Newtown & Machynlleth shed, on the right, is still in use. The lower yard on the left has a standard GWR 6-ton yard crane; and contains three GWR Toad brake vans, two of which are RU (Restricted use), taking up prime unloading spots. The narrow gauge Corris Railway station which was closed to passengers in 1931, and completely in 1948, was alongside to the left; the track was lifted in 1950. The two platforms at Machynlleth were offset and the Down platform only started where the photographer is positioned. In the right foreground is a GWR clerestory roofed coach in Departmental use, painted navy blue with its clerestory side lights painted (or felted) over. Next to it is a very unusual catch or trap point which has an additional rail. The East signal box which was decommissioned in 1960 is in the distance. The train arriving is headed by No. 75020, considered to be the best of the Oswestry's Standard Class '4' 4-6-0s, which was at the shed from new in November 1953 until August 1958 when it went to Chester West.

Collett '2251' 0-6-0 No. 2260 heading a westbound local on 3rd May 1958. It had been allocated to Machynlleth since February 1947 and was withdrawn from there in November 1961. The scale of the elaborate building on the Down side of the station is apparent in this view.

BR Standard Class '2' 2-6-0 No. 78002 arrives at Machynlleth with a westbound train in the 1950s. It is passing a waiting train on the siding in front of the goods shed, called locally Aberystwyth Road, that was used to hold coaches for Aberystwyth which had been detached from trains going forward to Pwllheli; they could quickly be moved into the Down platform once the Pwllheli train had left. The chimneys of the engine shed are above No. 78002's cab and the first coach of its train.

BR Standard Class '4' 4-6-0 No. 75003 piloting a 'Manor' on the Down 'Cambrian Coast Express' in 1963. It was in lined green and had a double chimney from May 1959. No. 75003 was transferred from Tyseley to Machynlleth in September 1962 but only stayed until October 1963 when it went to Yeovil Town. The first coach, still in 'chocolate and cream' when the remainder of the train was in maroon, is the unique mini-buffet 'Autobar' which had been added to the train at Shrewsbury. It replaced the Restaurant Car which was taken off the Down train at Wolverhampton and returned to Paddington on the Up service.

The background to this picture of BR Standard Class '4' 2-6-4T No. 80135 arriving at Machynlleth with the 4.0pm Shrewsbury to Aberystwyth train on 24th July 1963 shows the recent improvements made to the facilities there by British Railways. A new goods shed was built to concentrate freight traffic for onward delivery by road after several smaller depots in the area were closed. The new flat-roofed two-storey signal box visible above the cab of No. 80135 was a BR (Western Region) Type '37' design which replaced the 1890s built East and West boxes in March 1960. Note the crossover from the goods shed road shown in the earlier pictures has been removed. No. 80135 was built at Brighton in April 1956 and worked on the London, Tilbury & Southend line until the completion of its electrification in July 1962 when it moved to Shrewsbury, then on to Oswestry in January 1963 before returning to Shrewsbury in September 1964. It was bought from Woodham Brothers scrapyard by the North Yorkshire Moors Railway in 1973 and has been used on that line since then.
Brian Stephenson

Machynlleth shed

Machynlleth was the largest of three sheds, together with Aberystwyth and Pwllheli, which provided the motive power for the Cambrian Coast lines. It was on a narrow site behind the station tucked against a rock face on land carved out of the hillside. It was built in two sections, in 1863 and 1873, and was improved by the GWR in the 1930s. A new coaling stage was built in 1948 and a larger turntable installed to accommodate the 'Manor' class engines.

The shed was coded 89C from nationalisation until September 1963 and became 6F under the London Midland Region. It had sub-sheds at Aberayron, Aberystwyth, Portmadoc and Pwllheli. Though carrying 89C shed plates between fifteen and twenty locomotives were regularly allocated to Aberystwyth and four were shedded nightly at Pwllheli and five or six similarly out-stationed at Portmadoc. Machynlleth closed to steam in December 1966 but remained in use as a stabling point for Diesel Multiple Units.

In June 1950 its allocation of fifty-six engines comprised thirteen '90XX' 4-4-0s, two 'Manor' 4-6-0s, fifteen '45XX' 2-6-2Ts, fourteen '2251' 0-6-0s, one 'Dean Goods' 0-6-0, two '14XX' 0-4-2Ts, two '74XX' 0-6-0PTs, one '16XX' 0-6-0PT, three Cambrian Railways Class '15' 0-6-0s and the three Vale of Rheidol engines. This was virtually the same as in the final year before nationalisation.

A decade later, BR Standard engines had replaced the older classes and had made inroads into some of the later GWR designs. There were six 'Manor' 4-6-0s, three '45XX' 2-6-2Ts, eight '2251' 0-6-0s, three '43XX' 2-6-0s, one '74XX' 0-6-0PT, one '57XX' 0-6-0PT, three Vale of Rheidol 2-6-2Ts and two Stanier Class '3' 2-6-2Ts with six BR Standard Class '2' 2-6-0s, four Class '3' 2-6-2Ts and two Class '4' 4-6-0s.

Left: '90XX' 4-4-0 No. 9004 on shed with Cambrian Railways Class '15' 0-6-0 No. 849 behind, in around 1953. The rake of coal wagons on the 'Hoist Road' into the modern corrugated iron coaling plant includes a GWR 20-ton coal wagon with double doors. The main shed buildings are just visible in the background.

Below: A view from the west end of the yard with '74XX' 0-6-0PT No. 7417 alongside the water tank on 28th July 1961. Note the substantial buttressing of the tank; it appears that the original Cambrian Railway building suffered from subsidence or structural failure. The shed was actually two connected two-road buildings, the one nearest the camera dating from 1863 and the other from 1873. In 1932 the GWR replaced the roof and fitted new doors and frames. On shed are a Standard Class '4' 4-6-0, a Standard Class '2' 2-6-0 and a '2251' 0-6-0.

Machynlleth had a sizeable allocation of Collett '2251' 0-6-0s throughout the 1950s, although reducing by the end of the decade as BR Standard classes took over. No. 3209 on shed in August 1961 was actually allocated to Oswestry at that date although it was transferred to Machynlleth at the start of 1963 and ended its days there in June 1964.

Cemmes Road

BR Standard Class '4' 4-6-0 No. 75023 runs alongside the River Dovey near Cemmes Road on the 12.0pm Aberystwyth-Shrewsbury on 18th September 1954. It was new to Oswestry in December 1953 and stayed until September 1956 when it left for Swindon, although it returned to the Cambrian in 1962 at Machynlleth.

The young lad with his improved version Box Brownie has taken his picture of '90XX' 4-4-0s Nos.9004 and 9018 at Cemmes Road with the Talyllyn Railway AGM special from Paddington to Towyn on 27th September 1958. Both engines were allocated to Croes Newydd shed having been transferred there from Machynlleth. LM&SR 'Compound' 4-4-0 No. 41123 had brought the train from Paddington to Shrewsbury where the two 'Dukedog's took over. Cemmes Road station served the nearby village of Cemmaes Road, the railway using the anglicised spelling to avoid confusion with the station at Cemmaes on the Mawddwy Railway. The six miles long Mawddwy Railway was built to carry slate from Dinas Mawddwy to the Cambrian main line at Cemmes Road and after a chequered history was finally closed in 1952.

Commins Coch

BR Standard Class '4' 4-6-0 No. 75004 at Commins Coch after descending from Talerddig with a westbound express in 1963. It had been transferred to Machynlleth from Bath Green Park in the four weeks ended 3rd November 1962 and was fitted with a double chimney at Swindon in October 1962. As part of its programme of investment in the Cambrian during the 1930s, the GWR opened the halt at Commins Coch in October 1931.

Llanbrynmair

Two 'Manor' 4-6-0s from Aberystwyth shed cross at Llanbrynmair, No. 7821 *Ditcheat Manor* waits with an Aberystwyth to Oswestry goods as No. 7819 *Hinton Manor* approaches with the Down 'Cambrian Coast Express' on 19th August 1963. *Hinton Manor* was the last 'Manor' built by the Great Western Railway, emerging from Swindon in February 1939, and *Ditcheat Manor* was the second of the class built by British Railways, entering service in November 1950. Both went to Woodham's scrapyard at Barry in South Wales after they were withdrawn from Shrewsbury in November 1965, becoming two of the nine engines in the class of thirty which survived into preservation. After it was purchased from Woodham Brothers at Barry in 1973 No. 7819 worked on the Severn Valley Railway from 1977 following restoration there, and also ran on the national network; it is now on static display at The Engine House, Highley. No. 7821 was at Barry until 1981 and was restored to working order in 1998, running on several preserved railways until its boiler ticket expired. It was purchased by the West Somerset Railway Association and in 2010 went on loan to the Steam Museum in Swindon. After it was replaced there by '28XX' 2-8-0 No.2818 in 2018, No.7819 was moved less than a mile down the road to the McArthur Glen Designer Outlet where it is currently on display until sufficient funds can be raised for a full overhaul before it is returned to operate on the West Somerset Railway.

M.J. Fox/Rail Archive Stephenson

BR Standard Class '3' 2-6-2T No. 82003 approaches Llanbrynmair station as it assists a 'Manor' 4-6-0 on the climb towards Talerddig with an Up express in 1963. The tank engine will come off the train at the summit and return to Machynlleth for its next job.

Tyseley's No. 7823 *Hook Norton Manor* waits at a deserted Llanbrynmair with a westbound express in 1963. It had been transferred there from Machynlleth in November 1962. The strange dustbin-like object on the platform is actually a painted pipe section used as a planter. Note the drop in the middle of the platform which was bisected by a minor road and crossing.

Talerddig

The fourteen miles from Machynlleth to the summit 693 feet above sea level at Talerddig had a continuous up gradient culminating in two miles at 1 in 52 and a final mile at 1 in 56. This meant that most summer passenger workings had to be piloted and most freight workings banked; some weekend trains loaded to thirteen coaches. Classes used for pilot work were '2251' 0-6-0s, '45XX' 2-6-2Ts, Ivatt Class '2' 2-6-0s and in the early 1950s '90XX' 4-4-0s. At the summit the pilot engine would be uncoupled and put into the dead-end siding extension of the loop to await its return to Machynlleth. In the other direction there were broken gradients over the eight miles from Caersws, the steepest a half mile at 1 in 71 near Pontdolgoch station and culminating in three-quarters of a mile at 1 in 80 to the summit. Trains other than the Saturday 'Cambrian Coast Express', which had two engines working through from Welshpool to Machynlleth, were not usually assisted.

The 12.0pm Aberystwyth-Shrewsbury stopping train enters the loop at Talerddig headed by '90XX' 4-4-0 No. 9004 on 26th September 1953. It will turn off the Cambrian at Buttington, just beyond Welshpool, on to the ex-GWR and L&NWR Joint line to Shrewsbury. No. 9004 was built in August 1936 as No. 3204 *Earl of Dartmouth* from 'Duke' No. 3271 and 'Bulldog' No. 3439 and was renumbered as 9004 in July 1946.

One of the post-war Collett '2251' 0-6-0s, No. 3202 with an eastbound pick-up freight at Talerddig. It went to Oswestry from new in October 1946, moving to Machynlleth in October 1950. This picture was taken after No. 3202 returned to Oswestry in July 1955; it was withdrawn from there in June 1960.

'2251' 0-6-0 No. 2210 approaches Talerddig with an eastbound Class 'K' freight on 23rd August 1958. It was one of seven of the class shedded at Oswestry in late 1957 but left for Shrewsbury in November 1958. No. 2210 was the last '2251' to remain in service, withdrawn from Banbury in June 1965. The class was restricted to 160 tons over the Talerddig Incline whereas the 'Manor' and BR Standard Class '4' 4-6-0s which took over their freight duties were allowed up to 288 tons and up to eight coaches on passenger trains. Although the timings of this train differed by about fifteen minutes either way it was always known as the '2 o'clock goods'.

No. 7810 *Draycott Manor* arrives at Talerddig with the 2.30pm Aberystwyth to Oswestry train on 29th July 1959. It had moved a few weeks earlier from Gloucester Horton Road to Oswestry and remained there until December 1963, ending its days at Machynlleth in September 1964.

R.O. Tuck/Rail Archive Stephenson

Milepost 62, within ¾ mile of the summit, was at the end of two miles at 1 in 52 which were followed by a slight easing to 1 in 56 up to the top. An unidentified 'Manor' 4-6-0, probably No. 7822 *Foxcote Manor*, is working hard on an eastbound train in 1964. It was transferred from Oswestry to Machynlleth in December 1963 and was there until the shed closed in January 1965 when it left for Shrewsbury.

Caersws

'2251' 0-6-0 No. 2286 departs from Caersws in the mid-1950s on the Up 'Cambrian Coast Express' with the combined Aberystwyth and Pwllheli portions which had joined at Dovey Junction. It was at Machynlleth from August 1954 until October 1962, except for a few months at Oswestry from late 1954 until mid-1955. Although the class were primarily goods engines, a number were painted in lined green during 1957 reflecting their use on passenger duties such as this.

The signalman is about to collect the single line token from the fireman of Ivatt Class '2' 2-6-0 No. 46446 as it arrives at Caersws with the 4.35pm Newtown to Machynlleth train on 19th August 1963. The 'Mogul' had only recently arrived on the Cambrian, moving from Rugby to Machynlleth in May 1963. Caersws was the former terminus of the Van Railway, built in 1871 to carry lead from the mines at Van near Llanidloes to the Cambrian main line and closed in 1940.

M.J. Fox/Rail Archive Stephenson

BR Standard Class '4' 2-6-4T No. 80132 waits at Caersws with the 2.45pm Aberystwyth to Oswestry on 19th August 1963. It had arrived on the Cambrian in January 1963 after spending its early years on the London, Tilbury & Southend line until electrification was completed in June 1962. The station survived the threat of closure under the Beeching Plan as the notional rail link for Llanidloes after the closure of the Mid-Wales line and is still open today, the only station left between Newtown and Machynlleth.

M.J. Fox/Rail Archive Stephenson

Moat Lane Junction

The first station at Moat Lane, opened in 1859, was a short distance to the south-west of the later junction station. When the Machynlleth line opened in 1863, a new station was built in the 'V' of the junction to replace the original station. It had a single straight platform face for the Llanidloes (Mid-Wales) trains and a curved platform and an island platform was built on the curve, thus providing three platforms for trains to/from Machynlleth.

Although carrying express passenger headlamps, '90XX' No. 9015 waits at Moat Lane with a short pick-up goods on 24th August 1957. It was allocated the name *Earl of Clancarty*, but entered service as plain No. 3215 in October 1937. It was built from 'Bulldog' No. 3420 and 'Duke' No. 3262 and was renumbered as 9015 in September 1946. It moved to Machynlleth from Oxford in July 1956 and was withdrawn in June 1960. No. 9015 has tapered buffers, no top feed and non-standard cab windows inherited from its predecessor 'Duke'. Note the Automatic Train Control pick-up shoe below the buffer beam.
D.M.C. Hepburne-Scott/Rail Archive Stephenson

Churchward '43XX' 2-6-0 No. 6342 and a '2251' 0-6-0 arrive at Moat Lane Junction with a westbound train in around 1958. The 'Mogul' was built in March 1923 and was at Oswestry from October 1958 until November 1960. Note the GWR concrete signal post.

Highly polished for Aberystwyth's prestige duty, No. 7818 *Granville Manor* at Moat Lane Junction with the Down 'Cambrian Coast Express'. It was transferred to Machynlleth, Aberystwyth's parent shed, from Oxley in January 1960 and stayed there until withdrawal in January 1965. The weekday 'Cambrian Coast Express' took two hours 39 minutes to run the 81½ miles between Shrewsbury and Aberystwyth inclusive of stops at Welshpool, Newtown, Moat Lane Junction, Machynlleth where it was allowed just five minutes to remove the Pwllheli portion, Dovey Junction and Borth. This contrasted with the sharp timing of 121 minutes for the 110.6 miles between Paddington and Birmingham. Note the siding in the foreground has been re-laid with GWR Concrete 'pot' sleepers. This was a Second World War practice due to the shortage of sleepers, the 'pots' being cast at Taunton and spaced with metal ties. In the 1960s there were quite a few surviving in sidings on the Cambrian section, together with a few earlier pressed steel ones.

CHAPTER 8 - DOVEY JUNCTION TO MOAT LANE JUNCTION

No. 7819 *Hinton Manor* leaves Moat Lane Junction with an Aberystwyth to Crewe train on 18th September 1961. It was the second of the class to be allocated to the Cambrian, arriving at Oswestry in July 1943, three months after the first No. 7807 *Compton Manor*. The two engines were used primarily on passenger work between Whitchurch and Aberystwyth. After withdrawal in November No. 7819 was purchased from Woodham Brothers at Barry in 1973 and worked on the Severn Valley Railway from 1977 after being restored there, and also ran on the main line; it is now on static display at The Engine House, Highley.
M.J. Fox/Rail Archive Stephenson

9 – The Mid-Wales line: Moat Lane Junction to Three Cocks Junction

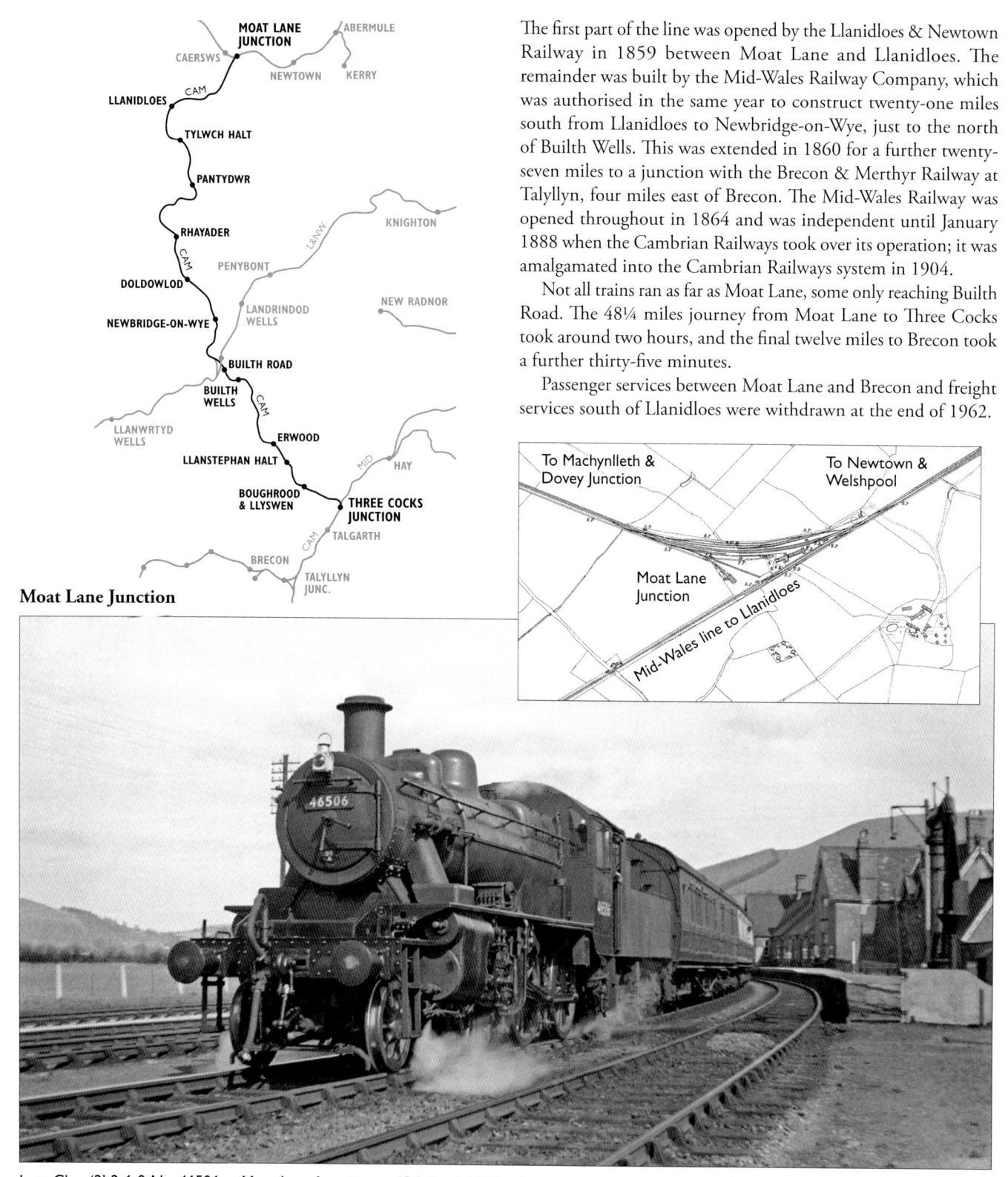

The first part of the line was opened by the Llanidloes & Newtown Railway in 1859 between Moat Lane and Llanidloes. The remainder was built by the Mid-Wales Railway Company, which was authorised in the same year to construct twenty-one miles south from Llanidloes to Newbridge-on-Wye, just to the north of Builth Wells. This was extended in 1860 for a further twenty-seven miles to a junction with the Brecon & Merthyr Railway at Talyllyn, four miles east of Brecon. The Mid-Wales Railway was opened throughout in 1864 and was independent until January 1888 when the Cambrian Railways took over its operation; it was amalgamated into the Cambrian Railways system in 1904.

Not all trains ran as far as Moat Lane, some only reaching Builth Road. The 48¼ miles journey from Moat Lane to Three Cocks took around two hours, and the final twelve miles to Brecon took a further thirty-five minutes.

Passenger services between Moat Lane and Brecon and freight services south of Llanidloes were withdrawn at the end of 1962.

Moat Lane Junction

Ivatt Class '2' 2-6-0 No. 46506 at Moat Lane Junction on 13th April 1955 is facing in the 'Down' direction towards Machynlleth with a train of non-corridor stock. However, it is possible that No. 46506 is propelling the stock back up the main line so that it can run forward into the Mid-Wales platform facing towards Llanidloes, a manoeuvre that took place regularly at this location.

Ivatt Class '2' 2-6-0 No. 46518 waits at Moat Lane Junction with a train to Brecon. This picture was taken between October 1959, when 46518 was transferred from Brecon to Oswestry, and January 1961 when Oswestry shed became 89D. The line stretching into the distance is to Newtown and Welshpool.

Llanidloes

'Dean Goods' 0-6-0 No. 2483 at Llanidloes with a southbound Mid-Wales line train on 29th August 1949. At this date, ex-Cambrian or ex-GWR 0-6-0s worked most of the traffic on the line. No. 2483 was built in 1896 and had three years left in service. It had been allocated to Oswestry since before nationalisation and was withdrawn from there. Llanidloes had an engine shed which was a sub-shed of Oswestry, and there were extensive freight facilities at the station including Up and Down refuge sidings, capable of holding an engine plus brake van and fifty wagons, and thirty-two wagons respectively.

Ivatt Class '2' 2-6-0 No. 46522 pulls into Llanidloes with a Brecon-Moat Lane train during the time it was allocated to Brecon, from March 1953 until October 1959. The disused South signal box is behind the engine and under the bridge is a very long headshunt – this is not a double track section as it may appear in this picture. All of the track south of Llanidloes was lifted by 1965, but the line to the north was given a new lease of life with the building of the Clywedog Dam, three miles from Llanidloes. It was used by cement trains from Aberthaw, in South Wales, which ran to Llanidloes via Shrewsbury. This traffic finished in 1967, and by October of that year Llanidloes had lost its rail link.

Tylwch Halt

The line climbed from Llanidloes to Tylwch at 1 in 75 for almost a mile, then levelling out before a climb at 1 in 60 at the steepest, for around half a mile, before reaching Tylwch Halt, which was originally a station with a passing loop. Ivatt 2-6-0 No. 46508 waits there with the 9.55am Moat Lane to Brecon train on 29th July 1959. It was transferred to Brecon from Oswestry in January 1955, replacing No. 46523 which went in the other direction. After Brecon shed was closed in November 1959 No. 46508 returned to Oswestry.

R.O. Tuck/Rail Archive Stephenson

CHAPTER 9 - THE MID-WALES LINE: MOAT LANE JUNCTION TO THREE COCKS JUNCTION

Pantydwr

Two trains cross at Pantydwr in 1959, with Ivatt Class '2' 2-6-0 No. 46518 on the southbound train to Brecon. Pantydwr was the highest station on the Cambrian, at 947ft above sea level and reached after a steep climb at 1 in 77. From there, the line descended towards St. Harmons and Marteg Tunnel.

Rhayader

A Builth Road to Moat Lane train at Rhayader headed by Cambrian Railways Class '15' 0-6-0 No. 893 on 29th August 1949. Built by Beyer, Peacock & Co. in March 1908 as Cambrian Railways No. 15, it was renumbered in October 1908 to No. 99 and rebuilt with a Swindon No. 9 superheated boiler in November 1924. It did not receive a BR smokebox plate and kept its buffer beam number until withdrawn in February 1953. Rhayader had a busy goods yard, as can be glimpsed in the background, with regular livestock fairs, a corn mill and a gas works generating freight traffic. The station was used by visitors to the nearby Elan Valley where there was a series of four dams on the Elan river built to supply water to the City of Birmingham.

'Dean Goods' 0-6-0 No.2538 is working hard up the incline near Rhayader with a northbound goods train on 9th October 1951. It was the last 'Dean Goods' in service, withdrawn on 15th May 1957 at Oswestry almost seventy years after it was built in August 1887. Their low axle loading allowed the 'Dean Goods' to work on the Mid-Wales line, which until 1940 was an 'uncoloured' route under the GWR route classification system, and they operated over it for more than a quarter of a century. At nationalisation almost half of the class remaining in service were on the Cambrian, retained primarily because they and the Cambrian Railways Class '15' 0-6-0s were the only tender engines permitted on the Mid-Wales Line and other weight restricted branches. When new Ivatt 2-6-0s were delivered at the end of 1952 a handful of 'Dean Goods' were retained to work on the branch lines where the 'Moguls' were prohibited. The last two were Nos. 2516 and 2538, allocated to Oswestry, which worked on the Kerry branch until its closure in 1956. The Railway Observer described their final months, 'the impending closure of the Cambrian Railways Kerry branch will soon render [both engines] redundant. The meagre traffic on this branch has required the leisurely attention of three trains per week for the past few years and is worked from Abermule by the engine and brakevan of the afternoon Oswestry to Newtown pick-up freight. 2516, still with yellow number on the buffer beam (a relic of RailTour working in the summer) worked the branch during the week ending 3rd December 1955, with 2538 having its weekly rest at Moat Lane shed. An early closure seems inevitable. After the termination of the freight train at Newtown, the " Dean" travels light to Moat Lane Junction, whence it takes the evening passenger train to Llanidloes and Brecon, returning to Oswestry the following day and repeating the process three times per week'.

J.I.C. Boyd, Neil Parkhouse collection

Doldowlod

With Gwasteddyn Hill on the right, 'Dean Goods' 0-6-0 No. 2351 heads a southbound goods train near Doldowlod in 1948. It was one of the earlier engines in the class, built in 1884, and was in service until February 1953. At this time there were five or six southbound freights each day over the Mid-Wales Line starting with the 3.40am train from Moat Lane Junction to Greenway Siding, just south of Talyllyn Junction, the 7.50am Moat Lane Junction-Llanidloes and the 9.30am Llanidloes to Brecon Yard, which is probably the subject of this photograph. In the afternoon an engine and van left at 2.35pm from Builth Wells to Llanelwydd Quarry Siding, and a cattle train ran on Talgarth Fair days at 4.10pm which went on to Merthyr, and finally a 6.00pm (as required) freight from Moat Lane to Builth Wells.

Newbridge on Wye

Ivatt Class '2' 2-6-0 No. 46518 with a southbound train to Brecon at Newbridge on Wye. The picture was taken in 1959 before 46518 was transferred from Brecon to Oswestry in October of that year.

Builth Road (Low Level)

At Builth Road (Low Level) the Mid-Wales Line was crossed by the former L&NWR Central Wales Line which had its own station, Builth Road (High Level) as described in Chapter 10.

A goods train on the Central Wales Line passes over the 2.45pm Moat Lane to Brecon hauled by Ivatt Class '2' 2-6-0 No. 46503 at Builth Road (Low Level) on 28th July 1959. It was the first of the class built at Swindon for the Western Region. The white painted building above the cab of No. 46503 is the refreshment room that served both lines and became the 'Cambrian Arms' public house which was open until 2018. The tall wooden structure above the first coach contained the lift used to transfer parcels and luggage between the two stations. Passengers had a ramp and steps to reach the High Level station, but had to cross between the two Low Level platforms using a barrow crossing. The running-in board advises passengers to 'CHANGE FOR LLANDRINDOD, LLANWRTYD, LLANCANNARCH & C.'; the suffix 'LOW LEVEL' was not added until after nationalisation. *R.O. Tuck/Rail Archive Stephenson*

Ivatt Class '2' 2-6-0 No. 46521 waits in the Low Level platform having come up from Brecon. This picture of the now-preserved 46521 on 15th August 1962 was taken from the High Level station. The Mid-Wales Railway station originally had only one platform with a timber waiting shelter, but by 1893 another platform was added for Up trains, together with a passing loop; the station buildings on the left of the picture were then built on the Down platform.

Ivatt Class '2' 2-6-0 No. 46507 is enveloped in steam on a cold winter's day in the late 1950s. It ended its days at Croes Newydd in June 1965 after leaving Oswestry in February 1963.

Builth Wells

The spa town of Builth Wells was one of four in the area – the other three having stations on the Central Wales line. In July 1951 the Royal Welsh Show, organised by the Royal Welsh Agricultural Society, was held at Builth Wells. It was the most expensive held up to that date, the show having been restarted in 1947 after the Second World War and brought a large number of visitors by rail.

The following three photographs were taken while the Show was open and its stands are visible in the background in two of them. The station was in Llanelwedd in Radnorshire but the town itself was in Breconshire on the opposite side of the River Wye, the county boundary running down the middle of the river.

The fireman of 'Dean Goods' No. 2449 prepares to collect the single line token from the Builth Wells signalman as it arrives from the north with visitors for the Show. Built in 1893 and Oswestry-allocated since May 1946, No. 2449 was withdrawn in January 1953, ousted by the new Ivatt 2-6-0s. *R.G. Turner*

Cambrian Railways Class '15' 0-6-0 No. 849 arrives at Builth Wells with a southbound Class 'K' local freight on 25th July 1951 as pedestrians returning from the Royal Welsh Show wait at the level crossing. It was one of the last three remaining Cambrian Railways' engines when withdrawn in October 1954, together with the other two survivors, Nos. 855 and 895. Note that half its chimney capuchon has rotted away. *R.G. Turner*

One of the non-auto fitted Collett 0-4-2Ts, '58XX' No. 5801, probably working a special to the Show. It had been allocated to Brecon's sub-shed at Builth Wells since it was built in 1932 but in December 1955 was replaced by an Ivatt 2-6-0, moving to Machynlleth where it worked the Barmouth-Dolgelley 'shuttle'. *R.G. Turner*

CHAPTER 9 - THE MID-WALES LINE: MOAT LANE JUNCTION TO THREE COCKS JUNCTION

Looking towards Builth Road with a train on the Central Wales line just visible in the right background, Ivatt Class '2' 2-6-0 No. 46521 at Builth Wells with a service to Three Cocks Junction and Brecon on 29th July 1961.

Erwood

In the 1940s and the early 1950s 'Dean Goods' 0-6-0s shared the Mid-Wales line duties with the Cambrian Railways Class '15' 0-6-0s. On 10th October 1950 No. 2401 heads a northbound passenger working near Erwood augmented from the usual two coaches with an additional coach and a horsebox at the rear. These engines had been permitted to work trains over this route from September 1926. No. 2401 had been allocated to Brecon from before nationalisation and was withdrawn from there in January 1953.

J.I.C. Boyd, Neil Parkhouse collection

From September 1926 the line between Moat Lane and Three Cocks was limited to a 14-ton axle-load, but in the 1930s the renewal of ex-Cambrian 72lb double-head rail began which would enable the line to become a 'Yellow' route, although the work was not completed until 1940. From December 1940, the 'Yellow' restricted Cambrian Railways' Class '15' engines were allowed to work between Moat Lane Junction and Brecon, subject to a speed restriction. Class '15' 0-6-0 No 855 heads a two-coach train from Moat Lane Junction to Brecon near Erwood on 10th October 1950. Built as Cambrian Railways No. 31 by Beyer, Peacock & Co. in May 1919 it was renumbered after it came into Great Western Railway ownership in 1923. The Class '15' was the last 0-6-0 design built for the Cambrian Railways and the first Cambrian engines to be built with Belpaire fireboxes. They were rebuilt by the Great Western Railway in the 1920s and 1930s with new boilers, all except one having the Standard No. 9 superheated boiler. No. 855 was the second to be modified, in October 1924, and with its brass safety-valve cover has the appearance of a Swindon product. It was the last of the class in service when withdrawn in October 1954 after new Class '2' 2-6-0s arrived on the former Cambrian system. No. 855 was allocated to Oswestry throughout its time under British Railways.

J.I.C. Boyd, Neil Parkhouse collection

Llanstephan Halt

Ivatt Class '2' 2-6-0 No. 46511 approaches Llanstephan Halt with the 1.20pm Brecon to Moat Lane Junction on Saturday, 4th August 1962. In the 1960s this was the August Bank Holiday weekend and so, in accordance with long-standing custom, the usual two-coach train had been augmented with a third vehicle even though the numbers travelling no longer really required such provision.
Robert Darlaston

Llanstephan Halt, one of several on the line opened by the Great Western Railway after the 1923 Grouping, had a short wooden platform and a small corrugated iron waiting shelter. The guard has checked the doors of the 1.20pm Brecon to Moat Lane Junction and is about to re-join No. 46511's train after a solitary lady passenger had alighted.
Robert Darlaston

Boughrood & Llyswen

Green-liveried Ivatt Class '2' 2-6-0 No. 46518 waits at Boughrood and Llyswen before departing for Brecon in April 1960. Boughrood was in Radnorshire and Llyswen, which was added to the station name in 1912, was in Breconshire. The spire of St. Cynog's Church, built in 1854, is in the background behind the 10mph permanent speed restriction sign.

Three Cocks Junction

At Three Cocks Junction the Mid-Wales Line met the former Midland Railway line from Hereford. The latter was built by the Hereford, Hay and Brecon Railway and opened in 1862 but only reached Three Cocks; the remaining twelve miles from Three Cocks to Brecon were owned by the Mid-Wales Railway and the Brecon & Merthyr Railway. The Midland Railway wanted access to the expanding industry of South Wales and agreed exclusive running powers over the Hereford, Hay and Brecon Railway in 1869, and took over the company in 1886. It reached Swansea in 1877 using running powers over the Brecon & Merthyr Railway, the company remaining independent until the 1923 Grouping when it became part of the GWR.

Three Cocks had a 'Y'-shaped layout, with the junction at the south end of the station although it was originally planned that there would also be a connection between the Mid-Wales and the Hereford, Hay and Brecon lines but this did not materialise and the land was sold off by 1880. The name of the station came from that of the nearby 15th century coaching inn rather than the adjacent but tiny village of Aberllynfi.

Three Cocks with Ivatt Class '2' 2-6-0 No. 46519 waits to depart with the 2.15pm to Hereford on 28th July 1959. The running-in board on the right was inscribed 'THREE COCKS CHANGE FOR BUILTH WELLS, LLANDRINDOD WELLS, LLANIDLOES, AND THE CAMBRIAN COAST.', the latter somewhat optimistically ignoring the need to change again at Moat Lane Junction after a two-hour journey up the Mid-Wales Line!   *R.O. Tuck/Rail Archive Stephenson*

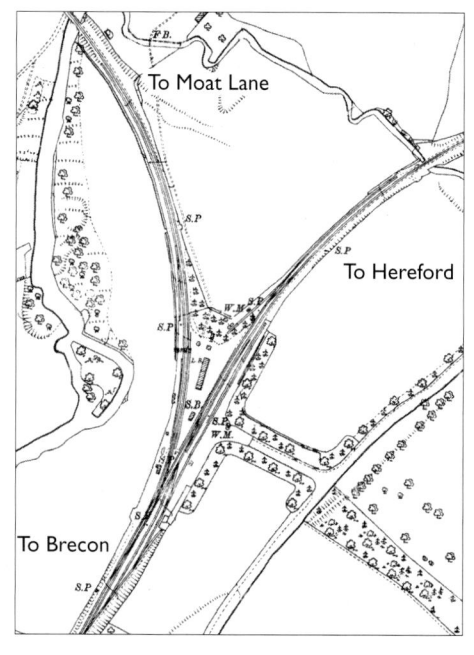

CHAPTER 9 - THE MID-WALES LINE: MOAT LANE JUNCTION TO THREE COCKS JUNCTION

Another picture of No. 46519 on the 2.15pm train to Hereford on 28th July 1959 shows the signal box and station building in the angle formed by the junction. The main station building was very similar on both sides, with identical door and window arrangements. The door with the sign above it led to the Refreshment Rooms; this was the same on both platforms. Unlike the running-in board, the signal box name board referred to the junction, namely 'THREE COCKS Jc. SIGNAL BOX'.
R.O. Tuck/Rail Archive Stephenson

The classic view of Three Cocks Junction at the western end with two Ivatt Class '2' 2-6-0s. On the line curving away to the left, No. 46523 had arrived from Moat Lane over the Mid-Wales line. In the platform on the right, No. 46518 had come from Hereford over the Hereford, Hay and Brecon Railway line. From 1953 onwards, the Ivatt 2-6-0s took over most of the workings on the Hereford line, which had been transferred to the Western Region in April 1950. Previously, it had been worked by Lancashire & Yorkshire Railway 0-6-0s, Midland Railway '3F' 0-6-0s and latterly 'Dean Goods' 0-6-0s. Local passengers had to use the barrow crossing over up to four running lines to access the platforms.
M. J. Brown collection

The Ivatt 2-6-0s worked not only on the passenger trains which passed through Three Cocks Junction but also most of the freight duties. No. 46513 runs through the passenger loop with a northbound freight for the Mid-Wales line on 9th June 1961.   *M.J. Brown collection*

The enclosed tender cabs of the Ivatt Class '2' 2-6-0s must have been very welcome for the engine crews who had previously 'enjoyed' the elements when working on this line tender-first with a 'Dean Goods' or other older classes. The design of the tender with the narrow tank also gave easy access to the coal space where the fireman of No. 46514 is holding a rather large lump of coal, and appears to be in need of a hammer, while working the 11.15am to Moat Lane Junction on 9th June 1961.   *M.J. Brown collection*

10 – The Central Wales line

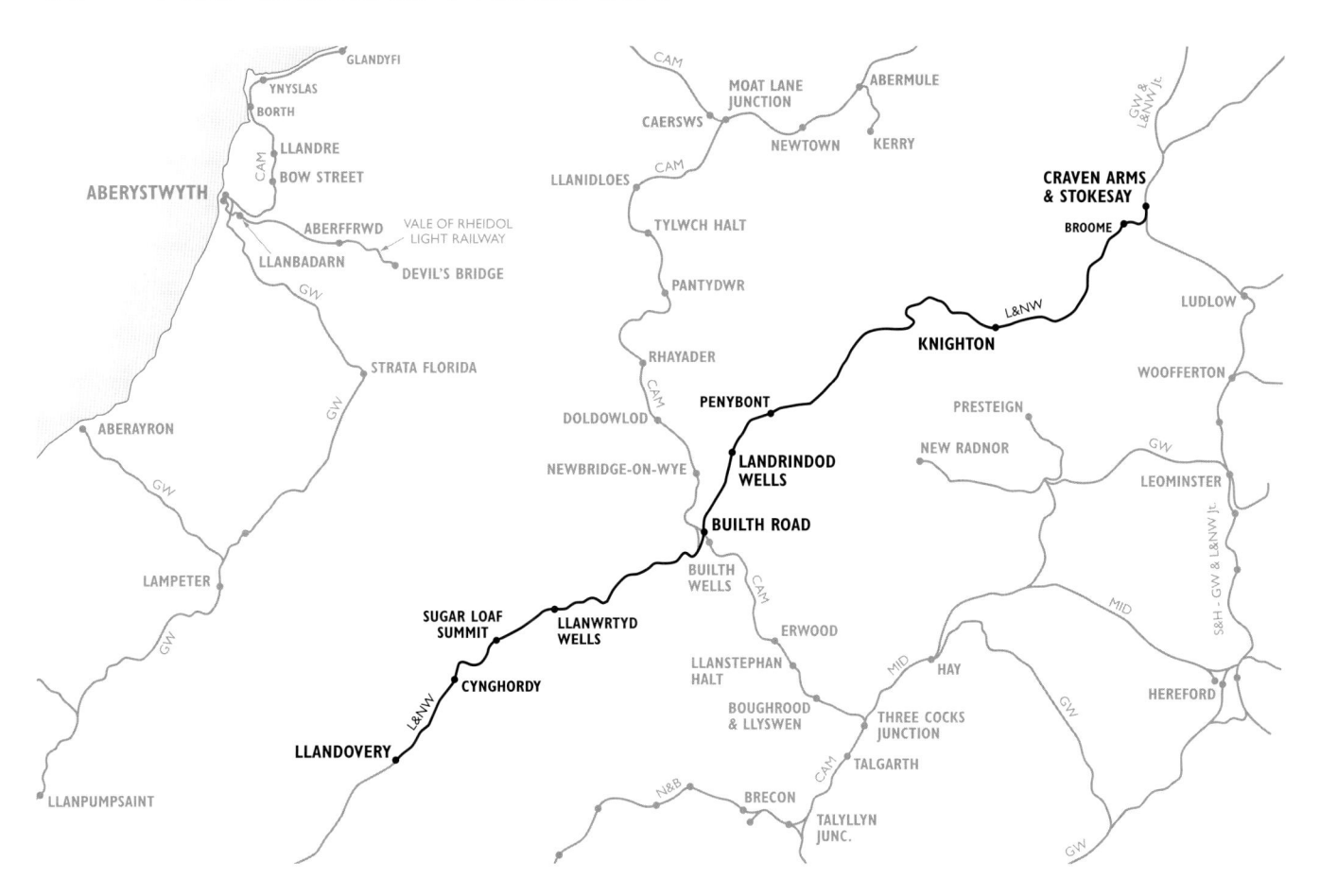

The Central Wales line between Craven Arms and Swansea Victoria was developed piecemeal by five separate companies and opened throughout in June 1868. Leaving Shrewsbury, trains first ran twenty miles over the northern half of the Shrewsbury & Hereford main line (joint London & North Western Railway and Great Western Railway) to Craven Arms and Stokesay. The Knighton Railway built the first twelve miles from there to Knighton, the Central Wales Railway the next twenty miles to Llandrindod Wells and the Central Wales Extension Railway the following 26¼ miles to Llandovery; all three were taken over by the L&NWR in 1868. At Llandovery it met the Vale of Towy Railway for the next twelve miles to Llandilo. This was originally leased to the other four companies involved in the line and eventually became the joint property of the L&NWR and the GWR in 1889. The final stretch to Swansea Victoria was built by the Llanelly Railway and initially leased by the L&NWR which then purchased it in 1873. The L&NWR having provided financial backing and engineering expertise, thus had its own route from North West England to South Wales, and one which was shorter by around fifty miles than the line via Hereford and Newport.

The whole of the Central Wales line was placed under the control of the Western Region at nationalisation in 1948 but little changed for the next fifteen years apart from a continuation of the decline in traffic which had started in the 1930s. Great Western engines such as 'Manor' 4-6-0s could not work over the northern end of the line because of width restrictions over their cylinders and so the ex-LM&SR engines continued on both through passenger and freight work until supplemented by BR Standards at the end of the 1950s.

A proposal in 1960 to install a Central Traffic Control system between Craven Arms and Llandovery from a new control centre at Llandrindod and eliminate most of the signal boxes was aborted and an attempt was made to close the whole line in 1962. This was strongly resisted and, in the event, only the section between Pontardulais and Swansea Victoria, including the latter station itself, was closed in June 1964. Services then ran to Swansea High Street via Pontardulais and the former Llanelly branch. Swindon 'Cross Country' diesel multiple units took over the passenger workings and through freight services ended; local freight was withdrawn in May 1965 although the yard at Llandovery remained open and was served from the south until the 1980s.

Craven Arms and Stokesay

The Central Wales line proper began at Craven Arms and Stokesay where it diverged from the Shrewsbury-Hereford line at Central Wales Junction running parallel with it for a short distance before turning westwards. It was a junction not only for the Central Wales Line but also for branches to Bishop's Castle and Much Wenlock, the latter connecting with the Severn Valley line at Buildwas. When the station opened in 1851 the immediate population was small and its name was taken from a coaching inn at the junction where four roads met; nearby was Stokesay Castle which provided the second part of the station's name. Craven Arms had an extensive goods yard, several private sidings and a locomotive depot which was a sub-shed of Shrewsbury. In May 1965 the line was singled to Knighton and the Central Wales junction signal box closed.

Left: A pair of Fowler '4P' 2-6-4Ts, Nos. 42385 and 42305, wait to leave Craven Arms with the 5.0pm Shrewsbury to Swansea Victoria on 15th June 1951. Swansea Paxton Street shed had six of these tanks, including No. 42385, from before 1948 until the depot closed at the end of August 1959 when they were transferred to Landore. They had been used on the Central Wales Line since the late 1920s, replacing the L&NWR Bowen-Cooke 4-6-2Ts. Still with LMS lettering on its tank sides three years after nationalisation, No. 42305 joined them in June 1948 and also stayed until 1959.

C.R.L. Coles/Rail Archive Stephenson

Right: Fowler '4P' 2-6-4T No. 42305 at Craven Arms in the late 1950s with a four-coach 'Ordinary Passenger' service to Swansea. 42305 had been transferred from Wigan Central to Swansea Paxton Street in June 1948, moving to Landore in August 1959 and then to Swansea East Dock in June 1961 from where it was withdrawn in August 1962. Note the banner repeaters for both Home and Distant signals; the latter were quite unusual. The lamp posts with their 'swan necks' are of GWR design, their square hanging lanterns having been replaced with Sugg gas lamps.

Left: Ex-L&NWR 'G2A' 0-8-0 No. 49113 and ex-Midland Railway '3F' 0-6-0 No. 43679 outside the Craven Arms sub-shed of Shrewsbury on 27th September 1957. No. 49113 was at Pontypool Road from October 1955 until withdrawn in January 1959 and No. 43679 was at Shrewsbury from pre-nationalisation days until February 1959. No. 49113 was built as a 'G' Class 0-8-0 No. 1634 in 1910, rebuilt to a superheated 'G1' with Belpaire firebox in 1933 and a 'G2A' with a 175lb per sq. in. boiler in 1939. The 0-8-0s worked on the Central Wales Line from before the 1923 Grouping until just before the closure of Paxton Street Shed, being finally withdrawn in April 1958. Two '3F' 0-6-0s were stationed at Craven Arms to work on alternate days the banking duty at Knighton. The one not employed on banking work took an early morning goods from Knighton, returning in the late afternoon replacing the L&NWR 'Coal Tank' 0-6-2Ts or Midland '2F' 0-6-0s on station pilot duties at Craven Arms. The sub-shed was closed when local freight services were withdrawn in May 1965.

R.O. Tuck/Rail Archive Stephenson

CHAPTER 10 - THE CENTRAL WALES LINE

BR Standard Class '5' 4-6-0 No. 73023 with a Swansea train at Craven Arms and Stokesay in the early 1960s. In 1960 the Standard '5's had displaced the Stanier Class '5's which had been used on the Central Wales Line expresses since the 1930s, but in 1963 the Stanier engines returned when other duties were found for the Standards. No. 73023 had moved to Llanelly from Cardiff Canton in May 1960 and stayed until June 1964 when it went to Bath Green Park. The large running-in board states 'CRAVEN ARMS AND STOKESAY JUNCTION FOR LLANDRINDOD WELLS AND CENTRAL WALES LINE TO SWANSEA (VICTORIA)', much simplified from earlier years when there was a large sign board describing the places for which there were direct services and connections, including Llandrindod Wells, Brecon, Llanelly, Swansea, Carmarthen, Pembroke Dock and the GWR routes to Much Wenlock, Wellington and Market Drayton.

Broome

BR Standard Class '5' 4-6-0 No. 73003 leaves Broome with the 7.50am Craven Arms to Swansea 'Ordinary Passenger' service on 20th August 1963. It had moved to Shrewsbury in March 1963 but left after six months going to Bristol Barrow Road. Note the L&NWR-pattern signal box and signal, complete with its corrugated steel arm. Its ladder, situated to the front of the post was a feature unique to the L&NWR amongst the major pre-grouping companies.
M.J. Fox/Rail Archive Stephenson

Knighton

Knighton was originally the terminus of the Knighton Railway and although serving a town in Radnorshire the station building lay within the borders of Shropshire. A boundary post at the Swansea end of the station platforms defined the border between England and Wales. Knighton was at the end of the first section of double track on the Central Wales line and had a small goods yard on the Down side and a layby for forty-five wagons. There was a single-road engine shed which was large enough for two locomotives; the engines, which came from Craven Arms shed, were mainly used for banking trains up to Llangunllo Summit.

BR Standard Class '5' 4-6-0 No. 73023 departs from Knighton on a Shrewsbury-Swansea service in around 1962. Although carrying express passenger headlamps, trains on the 115¼ miles from Shrewsbury to Swansea Victoria averaged around 4¼ hours, but only 3¾ hours in the opposite direction. The standard GWR tubular post signal has its arm fitted lower than usual for sighting purposes and the bridge plate No. 18 is headed 'L.&N.W. &G.W. Joint Lines'. The lineside huts are fascinating, the glazed and painted one looks like it was a former ground frame but the L&NWR provided standard sectional buildings so it could just be one of these. There is oil for lubrication in a barrel on a stand (lamp oil was usually kept in locked sheds) and the ladder is safely stowed on the substantial fence made from old sleepers. All of these would be the doing of the local Permanent Way line ganger who based himself in the huts.

The Stanier '8F' 2-8-0s began working the heaviest freight services on the Central Wales Line in 1937 although they did not oust the L&NWR 0-8-0s from other freight work. No. 48328 was departing from Knighton towards Knucklas on 28th April 1951. It was built at Crewe in 1944 and was allocated to Shrewsbury from before 1948 until late 1959 when it was transferred to Llanelly. No. 48328 is hauling a Class 'H' freight which originated from Coleham Yard at Shrewsbury and is being banked on the ten miles up to Llangunllo summit. The single line track ran literally alongside the garden walls of the houses here.

Pen-y-Bont

BR Standard Class '5' 4-6-0 No. 73025 near Pen-y-bont on the second section of double track on the Central Wales Line with a Shrewsbury to Swansea train on 5th April 1962. It was allocated to Shrewsbury from April 1959 until January 1965 when it moved to Oxley. Pen-y-bont was near the foot of the descent from Llangunllo and the station there was built on a falling gradient of 1 in 74. *D.M.C. Hepburne-Scott/Rail Archive Stephenson*

Llandrindod Wells

Llandrindod Wells was one of the three spa towns on the Welsh section of the line, and one of the busiest passenger stations. '4P' 2-6-4T No. 42305 waits there with a Shrewsbury-Swansea working. The Fowler engines moved to Landore when Swansea Paxton Street closed in August 1959, but their days on the Central Wales Line were coming to an end. One Fairburn and two Stanier 2-6-4Ts arrived at Landore on loan in November 1959 while three of the Fowler 2-6-4Ts were at Derby Works; two of the loanees left in April 1960 and the third in June. The Fowlers stayed on until mid-1962 when they were withdrawn after the arrival of BR Standard 2-6-4Ts displaced by the London, Tilbury & Southend electrification. Traffic at the station had declined by this date and the Up platform was taken out of use. Note the Southern Region-pattern concrete platform lamps.

BR Standard Class '5' 4-6-0 No. 73023 produces plenty of smoke for the camera as it sets off from Llandrindod Wells on a Shrewsbury-Swansea train in around 1962. It had moved to Llanelly from Cardiff Canton in May 1960 and stayed there until June 1964 when it went to Bath Green Park. In 1964 there were still four through trains between Shrewsbury and Swansea Victoria and another starting at Craven Arms; northwards there were five trains to Shrewsbury. Although the layout had long since been rationalised to a single track, the redundant Up platform canopy is still in place.

Builth Road (High Level)

Builth Road (High Level) station served Builth Wells although the spa town was over two miles away. Here, the Central Wales Line crossed over the Cambrian Railways' Mid-Wales Line at its Builth Road (Low Level) station (see Chapter 9). The two stations were connected for passengers by means of a ramp, steps and a luggage lift. Part of the High Level Up platform was built on a bridge over the Mid-Wales Line. There was a through road to the south west of the station connecting the two lines, with a small goods yard and L&NWR engine shed; it was lifted in 1969 over six years after the Mid-Wales line closed. For passengers, there was a refreshment bar and buffet on the Down platform of the Low Level station which was accessed by a ramp and steps. However, even during the heyday of the two lines there were no convenient connections for passengers changing trains. When the Mid-Wales line closed in December 1962, the 'Top Station' dropped its High Level suffix and it became an unstaffed halt in September 1965 when the passing loop was taken out of use.

Stanier '8F' 2-8-0 No. 48400 passes through Builth Road (High Level) with a northbound Class 'H' freight on 28th July 1959. This was the first of the Stanier engines built at Swindon Works during the Second World War, entering service in June 1943. It had been allocated to Swansea Paxton Street since March 1957 when it was transferred there from Toton. After the former shed closed in August 1959 No. 48400 moved to Llanelly before ending its days on the London Midland Region and lasting until the end of BR steam in August 1968. The running-in board advises passengers to 'CHANGE FOR BUILTH WELLS BRECON RHAYADER AND LLANIDLOES'. The tall wooden building on the left housed a water-powered lift to transfer parcels and luggage between the two stations.
R.O. Tuck/Rail Archive Stephenson

Fowler '4P' 2-6-4T No. 42305 pauses at Builth Road (High Level) on a southbound service in the late 1950s. Water cranes were provided at the ends of both the Up and Down platforms; the one here appears to be an improvised LM&SR (possibly wartime) design.

BR Standard Class '5' 4-6-0 No. 73023 at Builth Road (High Level) on a southbound express in the early 1960s. In the background is the goods shed and yard and there was also a passenger bay at the Llandrindod end of the station. The planked section of platform is on the bridge over the Mid-Wales line below.

Llanwrtyd Wells

Llanwrtyd Wells was near the top of a long climb at rising at 1 in 80, then at 1 in 100, and the stretch of track there was the longest on the level throughout the whole route. It was followed immediately by the continuous three mile ascent to Sugar Loaf Summit. Fowler '4P' 2-6-4T No. 42305 waits there with a southbound train in the late 1950s, before it was transferred to Landore in August 1959.

With its high-visibility headlight provided due to the number of level crossings on the line, a three-car Swindon 'Cross-Country' DMU and a Metro-Cammell two-car unit wait at Llanwrtyd Wells in the early 1970s. The 'Cross-Country' sets, Class '120' under TOPS, had worked on the Central Wales Line since the end of steam in 1964 and lasted until the mid-1980s when they were replaced by Metro-Cammell units. Initially the trains from Shrewsbury terminated at Llanelly and passengers had to change there for Swansea High Street, but from May 1970 through trains were re-introduced, reversing at Llanelly. The original station building has survived although it has lost its canopy, and the passing loop is still in use.

CHAPTER 10 - THE CENTRAL WALES LINE

Sugar Loaf Summit

Sugar Loaf Summit is 820 feet above sea level at the top of steep inclines in either direction, 1 in 70 from Llanwrtyd Wells and 1 in 60 from Llandovery. Freight trains had to halt at a 'Stop Board' so that the guard could check the train and the brakes on the wagons pinned down to control the speed downhill.

The signalman at Sugar Loaf Summit box makes his way down the steps to meet Shrewsbury '8F' 2-8-0 No. 48724 on a westbound freight. No. 48724 was allocated to Shrewsbury between 1955 and 1962. This was its fifth number; it was built by the L&NER at Brighton Works in 1944 as No. 7670, renumbered to 3119 in 1946 and then twice during 1947, firstly to 3519 and then into the LM&SR series as 8724 before finally gaining its BR number in 1948. *J. Suter collection*

The signalman at Sugar Loaf Summit box exchanges tokens with the fireman of green-liveried BR Class '5' 4-6-0 No. 73024 working the 12.0 mid-day Shrewsbury to Swansea train on 25th May 1962. No. 73024 was in its second spell allocated to Shrewsbury, from April 1960 until July 1962. Hidden behind the signal box and the train are two short platforms used by the ganger and signalmen's families, who lived in the three railway cottages there, to join trains to reach the nearby towns. Although the cottages are long since demolished and the platforms closed in 1965, the halt was re-opened in 1984 as a request stop, accessed via the steps on the left of the picture. *R.O. Tuck/Rail Archive Stephenson*

Cynghordy

'G2A' 0-8-0 No. 48893 approaches Cynghordy station on a northbound freight with the tall chimney of Cynghordy Brickworks in the background on 17th July 1953. This engine started life as a L&NWR Class 'B' four-cylinder compound 0-8-0 in 1902, numbered 2563, though it is doubtful if much of the original engine remained at this date other than the wheel centres and possibly part of the frames. It was fitted with a leading pony truck in 1908, becoming Class 'E'. In 1924 it was converted from compound to 'simple' operation and reverted to the 0-8-0 wheel arrangement as a superheated Class 'G1' with Belpaire firebox; it changed its number twice more, to No. 9604 in 1927 and then No. 8893 in 1930. Finally, in 1941, it was modified to a 'G2A' with a 175lb per sq.in. boiler in which condition it was in service until October 1954.
J. Suter collection

After nationalisation, Stanier Class '8F' 2-8-0s were often used on Central Wales passenger work. Swindon-built No. 48409 at Cynghordy on a southbound train had only arrived on the Central Wales line in February 1958 and by this date had been transferred from Swansea Paxton Street to Llanelly. It left for the Somerset & Dorset at Bath Green Park in August 1964 and was withdrawn there in 1965. Cynghordy was around two-thirds of the way down the 1 in 60 from Sugar Loaf Summit and the station had a single passenger platform and a small goods yard. The Midland Railway pattern signal box was installed by the LM&SR when a passing loop was added in 1929 to increase capacity on the line since before then there was no loop on the single line between the Summit and Llandovery. On the Up line stands a freight inevitably banked by another '8F', the crew of which are chatting in the 'four foot' before proceeding.

CHAPTER 10 - THE CENTRAL WALES LINE

Stanier '8F' 2-8-0 No. 48738 heads a northbound Class 'H' freight away from Cynghordy in late-1963 or 1964, given the lowered top lamp iron on the smokebox door. Despite its modest train it still requires a banker from Llandovery up the 1 in 60 incline to Sugar Loaf Summit. Built to L&NER orders as Class 'O6' at Darlington in December 1945 numbered 3133, it was renumbered as 3533 in March 1947, then to No. 8738 in October 1947 when loaned to the LM&SR before finally becoming No. 48738 in April 1950. It moved to Shrewsbury at the end of 1952 and was there until September 1964.

Also with banking assistance, Stanier 'Jubilee' 4-6-0 No. 45699 *Galatea* with a northbound train at Cynghordy, some time after September 1963 when Shrewsbury shed became 6D. It had moved there from Bristol Barrow Road in September 1961 after 'Peak' diesels arrived and stayed until withdrawn in November 1964. *Galatea* was rescued from Barry scrapyard, but with part of one middle driving wheel cut-off following a mishap when being moved in Woodhams' yard. Although most parts which could be removed for use on classmate No. 45690 *Leander* had been stripped off, it was moved in 1980 to Carnforth although restoration was then not attempted because of the prohibitive cost. By 1992 the remains were moved again, to Kidderminster on the Severn Valley Railway, originally to provide a spare boiler for *Leander*. In 2002 *Galatea* was sold to the West Coast Railways and moved to Steamtown Carnforth where it was completely rebuilt, including the manufacture of a new driving wheel. No. 45699 returned to steam in April 2013 and made its railtour debut in May 2013 working a private charter from King's Lynn to Norwich; it is currently operating on the main line.

Llandovery

Llandovery marked the end of the L&NWR-owned line from Craven Arms, the following section being jointly owned with the GWR. It originally had two engine sheds, a four-road building built by the L&NWR in 1901 which housed eight engines and was a sub-shed of Swansea Paxton Street, and a small single-road GWR shed which closed in 1935. The L&NWR shed continued in use until the withdrawal of steam traffic from the line in August 1964. It provided banking engines for the climb up to the Sugar Loaf summit to the north.

The ganger is attending to a trolley and does not look up at Fowler '4P' 2-6-4T No. 42305 as it departs from Llandovery past the goods shed on a Shrewsbury-Swansea 'Ordinary Passenger' train in the mid-1950s.

There is an unusual double pole apparatus on the right for the token exchange but the signalman prefers to collect it himself from Stanier '8F' 2-8-0 No. 48452 as it approaches Llandovery No. 1 signal box with a very short southbound trip freight off the single line from Cynghordy. Built at Swindon in September 1944, No. 48452 arrived on the Central Wales Line in February 1958 at Swansea Paxton Street along with No. 48409 and was at Llanelly when this picture was taken, probably in 1962.

CHAPTER 10 - THE CENTRAL WALES LINE

BR Standard Class '5' 4-6-0 No. 73023 leaves Llandovery with a Shrewsbury-Swansea 'Express Passenger' in 1962. Llandovery shed had twenty-five sets of footplate crew in the early 1960s although it had only four duties of its own of which two were banking up to Sugar Loaf. This was because the station was a relieving point for men from Shrewsbury going south and Swansea or Llanelly going north and nearly all trains changed crews there.

A schoolgirl in a boater hat is looking out of the carriage droplight at an '8F' waiting to move off across the level crossing. '56XX' 0-6-2T No. 5604 stands at the north end of Llandovery station in 1962. Built at Swindon in January 1925, No. 5604 was allocated to Llanelly from September 1961 until withdrawn in December 1962 and was probably working the daily school train which ran between Llandovery and Llangadog.

Swindon-built Stanier '8F' 2-8-0 No. 48409 with a three-coach 'Ordinary Passenger' at Llandovery in 1962, a working that in earlier years would have had a Fowler 2-6-4T. No. 48409 was transferred in February 1958 from Hereford to Paxton Street and moved to Llanelly in August 1959 when the Swansea shed closed. Note the internal use van standing by the buffer stops outside the goods shed, no doubt providing additional covered storage. It was an early LM&SR design dating from the mid-1920s and built mostly by outside contractors.

11 – Moat Lane Junction to Welshpool

The Oswestry and Newtown Railway opened its line between Oswestry and Welshpool in August 1860 and reached Newtown in June 1861. The section from Newtown to Moat Lane Junction was opened by the Newtown and Machynlleth Railway in 1863. Both companies were absorbed into the newly formed Cambrian Railways in July 1864.

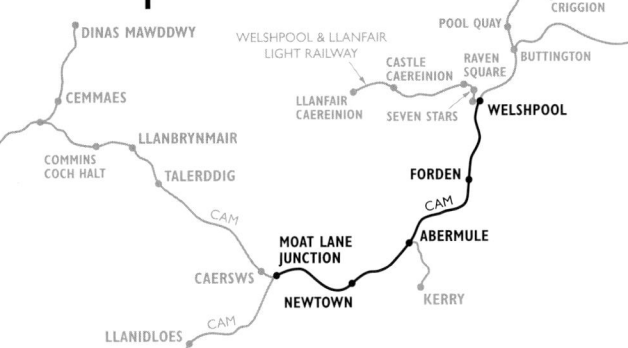

Newtown

No. 7823 *Hook Norton Manor* at Newtown with a westbound excursion from the Midlands in 1963. It had been transferred from Machynlleth to Tyseley in November 1962 and was withdrawn from the Birmingham shed in July 1964. The large building prominent in the background is the Royal Welsh Warehouse, opened in 1886/7 and Grade II listed in 1988. It was built by Sir Pryce Pryce-Jones, a draper in the town who founded the world's first mail order business in 1859. He produced a product catalogue, selling nationally and internationally, and the goods were despatched from Newtown by rail.

BR Standard Class '3' 2-6-2T No. 82009 pre-heating the coaches of the afternoon school train to Machynlleth in 1964. It had been transferred from Bristol St. Philip's Marsh to Machynlleth in February 1961. Most of the Western Region members of the class were repainted in green from 1957 including No. 82009 which was dealt with in May of that year with GWR-style orange/black/orange lining. This bay platform was originally the Llanidloes branch bay, but after the first few years most Llanidloes trains started from Moat Lane.

Abermule

'43XX' 2-6-0 No. 6335 at Abermule with a northbound train on 27th May 1958. It had been on the Cambrian since June 1956 when it was transferred from Landore, firstly to Oswestry and then almost immediately to Machynlleth. Abermule was the junction with the 3¾ mile long Kerry branch which had closed to passengers in 1931 although goods services continued until May 1956. The main line goods services were withdrawn in May 1964 and following the Beeching Plan's recommendations, Abermule station closed in June 1965.

Forden

BR Standard Class '4' 2-6-4T No. 80099 at Forden near Welshpool on an eight-coach Shrewsbury-Aberystwyth train at Forden in July 1964. These large tank engines worked alongside their 4-6-0 equivalents on the heavier duties. Although a former London, Tilbury & Southend engine it followed a different path to the Cambrian than some of the other 2-6-4Ts displaced, moving briefly to Old Oak Common for storage, then to Swansea (East Dock) before reaching Machynlleth in July 1963; after withdrawal in May 1965 it was scrapped by G.Cohen at Morriston.

Welshpool

Welshpool Down yard showing all that remained of the engine shed built in 1861 by the Oswestry & Newtown Railway and demolished around 1935. Locomotives continued to be serviced in the open there until 1954, and the turntable and water tower remained in use until the end of steam.
No. 7803 *Barcote Manor* pauses to replenish its tender tank on 13th June 1956. It was one of the first 'Manors' on the Cambrian, transferred to Aberystwyth from Neyland in April 1946. Although recorded after nationalisation as a Machynlleth engine it was actually allocated to the Aberystwyth sub-shed for more than a decade. Note the new sectional concrete agricultural store in front of the gas works on the site of the former timber yard.

Down trains at Welshpool used an island platform; the side nearest the goods yard was normally used for trains arriving from Shrewsbury, and the Down main on the left for through trains. BR Standard Class '4' 4-6-0 No. 75024 waits on a westbound service in around 1956. It was one of the third batch of the class built at Swindon that were originally intended for the London Midland Region but were instead allocated to the Western Region, the three sent to Oswestry displacing 'Manor' class 4-6-0s. No. 75024 was one of these, and stayed there from new in December 1953 until February 1958 when it moved to Shrewsbury. The yard is busier than in the previous picture with a British Road Services lorry, two 'piggy-backed' trailers, a flat-bed truck and a van to the right of the standard GWR hand crane.

A group of youngsters stand near Oswestry's No. 7819 *Hinton Manor* at Welshpool as it waits for departure time with an Up train in the mid-1950s. It went from new in February 1939 to Carmarthen, then moved to Oswestry in 1943, remaining there for most of its working life but ending its days at Shrewsbury from January 1965. *Hinton Manor* was sold to Woodham's at Barry but has survived into preservation, spending most of its time since then on the Severn Valley Railway. Note the attractive ironwork on the end of the Up platform awning which contrasts with the plain wooden end on the Down platform awning.

CHAPTER 11 - MOAT LANE JUNCTION TO WELSHPOOL

A busy time at Welshpool with three of the four platforms occupied. '43XX' 2-6-0 No. 6347 is in the Up Main platform and BR Standard Class '4' 2-6-4T No. 80102 waits in the Up bay platform. This bay was usually allocated for local trains starting for Shrewsbury, but local trains for Oswestry and Whitchurch which started at Welshpool also used it. The Churchward 'Mogul' was built in April 1923 and was allocated to Carmarthen from October 1961 until its final posting to Llanelly in June 1962; it was withdrawn at the end of 1963. The Standard tank was on the London, Tilbury & Southend from new in 1955 until July 1962 moving to Old Oak Common then Shrewsbury in November 1962 and finally to Bangor in January 1965. Its 89A shed plate suggests this picture was probably taken in mid-1963.

The fireman of No. 7803 *Barcote Manor*, watched by the driver, puts the water column bag back in place as it waits with a Down express. It has a 6F Machynlleth plate which dates this picture after September 1963. Although the train does not have a 'Cambrian Coast Express' headboard, its engine is one of those specially prepared by Aberystwyth shed for its prestige duty with the use of silver paint on the buffers and smokebox door ironwork. It is interesting that, although Welshpool was not actually a junction, the running-in board on the left states 'WELSHPOOL JUNCTION FOR SHREWSBURY, STAFFORD, BIRMINGHAM, LONDON', recognising that many passengers changed trains there; the lines from Oswestry and Shrewsbury joined at Buttington two miles to the north of the station. In the background, the large and elaborate French Renaissance style station building is today used as a retail outlet and passengers have to make do with basic station shelters. It was constructed using orange/red bricks with stone dressing and had six intermediate bays flanked by two pyramidal towers, each three floors high. It was a very large building for the size of the town it served, reflecting the intention to accommodate the Oswestry & Newtown Railway offices.

The fireman climbs back into the cab and the signal is off for No. 7819 *Hinton Manor* to depart towards Buttington Junction where it will either head north towards Oswestry or east to Shrewsbury. Welshpool was re-signalled in 1897 and two L&NWR-design signal boxes were provided. Welshpool South box was located at the south end of the up platform. It controlled the southern end of the station and the single line section that ran southwards to Forden. Welshpool North box was located to the north of the goods shed on the west side of the main line. It controlled the north end of the station and the connections with the goods yard and locomotive shed. It was provided with an L&NWR Tumbler locking frame but this was replaced by a second-hand Dutton frame, with standard GWR 5-bar tappet interlocking, after the South box was closed in 1931, and the North suffix dropped. The raised metal structure on the front of the tender was an early Health and Safety device fitted to engines likely to appear 'under the wires' at electrified stations, in this case at Crewe, as a reminder to the fireman to be very careful both when climbing onto the coal and when handling fire irons and tools.

CHAPTER 11 - MOAT LANE JUNCTION TO WELSHPOOL

BR Standard Class '4' 2-6-4T No. 80132 leaves Welshpool with the 12.35pm Aberystwyth to Whitchurch train on 22nd July 1963 having left the two coaches for Shrewsbury in the platform. Originally a London, Tilbury & Southend engine until July 1962 it moved to Oswestry in January 1963 before going to Bangor in January 1965. From the gentleman in these two shots it was obviously necessary to carry a raincoat in this part of Wales in mid-July!
Brian Stephenson

Ivatt Class '2' 2-6-0 No. 46505 has collected the Shrewsbury coaches and follows the 2-6-4T out. Although it has an 89D Oswestry shed plate, it had been transferred from there to Willesden in March 1963 and then to Chester in May, neither shed having replaced the Oswestry shed plate by the date of this picture.
Brian Stephenson

A two-coach Down 'Ordinary Passenger' service approaches Welshpool station headed by No. 7827 *Lydham Manor* which is emitting an excessive amount of black smoke. It has a 6F Machynlleth shedplate dating this as post-December 1963 when No. 7827 was transferred there from Oswestry. The L&NWR-design signal box has a painted name 'Welshpool Signal Box' rather than the usual GWR cast iron variety.

An unidentified BR Standard Class '4' 4-6-0 sets off from Welshpool in 1965. This, from the uniform set of BR Mark 1 coaches, may be the Up 'Cambrian Coast Express'. In the summer of 1965 a regular duty for the four Class '4' engines at Shrewsbury, Nos. 75014/38/53/63, was a daily 325 mile double return trip to Aberystwyth. This consisted of the 4.10am York mail from Shrewsbury, the Up 'Cambrian Coast Express' (9.50am from Aberystwyth), the Down 'Cambrian Coast Express' (2.30pm from Shrewsbury) and finally the 6.10pm York mail back to Shrewsbury. The Standard 4-6-0s had taken over the working from the GWR 'Manor's from mid-November 1965 and the last Up 'Cambrian Coast Express' on 4th March 1967 was hauled by No. 75033 and the final Down working by No. 75021.

12 – Welshpool & Llanfair Light Railway

In 1862 the first scheme was put forward for a railway linking Welshpool with the busy market town of Llanfair Caereinion, but this proposal for a standard gauge line was dropped as uneconomic. In 1864 plans were drawn up for a narrow gauge line but this too failed to gain sufficient support. There were further attempts over the next three decades, but none were successful until after the Light Railways Act, which simplified the legal requirements, became law in 1896. A Light Railway Order was issued in 1899 for the construction of a nine miles long 2ft 6in. gauge line, the Welshpool and Llanfair Light Railway, and negotiations were completed with the Cambrian Railways for a ninety-nine year undertaking whereby the W&LLR would provide the rolling stock and the Cambrian would build and maintain the line. The latter would work the line at its own expense and pass 40% of the gross traffic receipts to the W&LLR. When the Cambrian made a detailed estimate of the construction costs it was clear that further funds were needed and these were raised from a number of sources, including government grants and loans. However, the original plans had to be cut back with the number of locomotives reduced from three to two and similarly with the rolling stock. Construction started in 1901 and the line finally opened to freight traffic on 9th March 1903 and to passengers on 4th April. Almost inevitably, revenue failed to live up to expectations and in the twenty years up to 1923, when the Great Western Railway took over responsibility for the line, the investors and the exchequer both suffered losses. In 1925 the GWR started a motor bus service between Welshpool and Llanfair, and this was a prelude to the cessation of passenger traffic in February 1931, although goods traffic continued for another twenty-five years.

Although nationalisation in 1948 brought about little change, the future of the line was bleak, particularly because both engines needed major repairs and road vehicles had taken over most of the remaining traffic, especially with the need for transhipment to the main line at Welshpool. By the summer of 1950 closure was under consideration and although there was opposition from local councils, the final train ran on 3rd November 1956.

Fortunately, enthusiasts had been discussing the possible acquisition of the line since around 1952, following the example of the Talyllyn Railway two years earlier, and there were initial discussions with British Railways during that year. By 1956, the Ffestiniog Railway had also been saved and moves to purchase the W&LLR restarted. After overcoming a range of issues, the Preservation Society reached agreement with BR in 1959 to take over the line from Llanfair to Raven Square. It was to be leased over forty-two years and the rolling stock was made available on a hire purchase arrangement over ten years. In April 1963, exactly sixty years after the original opening ceremony, the line was re-opened in the presence of the Earl of Powis whose ancestor had been instrumental in the promotion of the railway at the end of the 19th century and whose name and that of his wife were carried by the two locomotives. The Welshpool town section was purchased by Welshpool Borough Council and after a 'Last Train' headed by both engines ran in August 1963, track lifting began although it was not completed until November 1965. The Preservation Society managed to purchase the line outright in 1974 but it would not be until 1981 that a new Welshpool terminus was opened at Raven Square.

Nos. 823 *Countess* and 822 *The Earl* outside the shed at Welshpool on 15th May 1954. No. 823 has a 'W' suffix to the number (below the cast plate) applied in 1948 but No. 822 did not have this. Note the 89A Oswestry shedplate; Welshpool was a sub-shed. Both engines were repainted in unlined green at Swindon in 1948, replacing the unlined black which had been their livery during World War Two. The original nameplates went to Swindon for safe keeping in 1951; those here are probably replicas or were loaned for the occasion, which was a visit by the Gloucestershire Railway Society. The two engines were 0-6-0Ts built by Beyer, Peacock & Co. Ltd in September 1902 as Cambrian Railways Nos. 1 and 2. They had outside frames, 2ft 9in. diameter wheels and Walschaerts valve gear operating 11½in. × 16in. outside cylinders. They were maintained at Oswestry Works and both were rebuilt at Swindon in 1930 with new boilers and standard GWR fittings including copper capped chimneys and brass safety valve covers, by which date they were GWR Nos. 822 and 823. As the line neared the end of its days under British Railways' ownership, both engines were unserviceable. No. 822 went to Oswestry for minor repairs in February 1956, returning five weeks later, but No. 823 never worked again and was sent to Oswestry for storage in March, and was joined in May 1958 by No. 822 which had been in Welshpool shed since the line closed in November 1956. In 1961 work commenced on their overhaul after a purchase price had been agreed with the Western Region by the Preservation Society. No. 822 was the first to be returned to service and arrived at Welshpool in July 1961; No. 823 remained under repair until 1962 and only returned in October. Note on the left the standard gauge GWR Iron Mink fitted with windows and grounded as additional storage space.   *Rail Archive Stephenson*

A goods train arriving at Welshpool crosses Church Street which was part of the main A483 road through the town; St. Mary's Church is in the background. This stretch of line was discontinued in preservation days when Welshpool Borough Council decreed that the new company could only work trains to a terminus at the south-west side of Raven Square. The fireman has left the footplate and displays his red flag as he signals the train across Church Street; he would also have done this at Raven Square and Union Street. The site is still recognisable today, the Tourist Information Centre being just to the right of the picture.

Rail Archive Stephenson

No. 822 standing alongside Smithfield Road on the west side of Welshpool station with a mixed goods train on 10th September 1951. In the left centre background is Welshpool Junior School, now Ysgol Maesydre, which gained Grade II Listed status in 2018. *Rail Archive Stephenson*

CHAPTER 12 - WELSHPOOL & LLANFAIR LIGHT RAILWAY

No. 822 climbs the bank to Canal Bridge immediately after leaving the yard in Welshpool with a goods train on 10th September 1951. The line crossed over the Shropshire Union Canal on a single 33ft 4in. span girder bridge before crossing the A483 Church Street and diving through a gap between the buildings and alongside shops and cottages to emerge at the site of the present-day Raven Square station.
Rail Archive Stephenson

No. 823 *Countess* holds up the traffic as it crosses the Brook Street/Raven Street junction with a train of nine open wagons from Llanfair in 1949. There was originally a halt at Raven Square on the town side of this intersection and today's preserved railway terminates there. The new station was opened in 1981 and several years later the railway purchased and re-erected the station building from Eardisley on the former Hereford, Hay & Brecon line. At the end of the Second World War both engines were in very poor condition with badly corroded fireboxes and worn tyres and in December 1946 No. 823 was deemed unfit for service. It was sent to Swindon for a complete overhaul including a new firebox and over a year later, in February 1948, it returned with its wartime unlined black livery replaced by unlined green. While *Countess* was away, No. 822 *The Earl* failed completely and had emergency repairs which enabled it to carry on the service within two weeks and once No. 823 was back it also went to Swindon for a major overhaul. The lodge on the extreme right was the gate lodge for the early 19th century Llanerchydol Hall and is now in use as holiday accommodation trading as Llanerchydol Lodge. It was given Grade II Listed status in 1981 'for its historical and architectural connection with Llanerchydol Hall, and as an example of a Picturesque Gothic lodge'; the Hall itself was listed in 1950.

W.B. Wilson/Rail Archive Stephenson

CHAPTER 12 - WELSHPOOL & LLANFAIR LIGHT RAILWAY

Castle Caereinion

No. 822 with a goods train including four loaded cattle wagons returning to Welshpool at Castle Caereinion on 10th September 1951. This was around halfway between Welshpool and Llanfair. It had a passing loop and the small signal box shown in this picture, but it had fallen into disuse by the 1930s and ground frames were installed to work the loop as a siding. *Rail Archive Stephenson*

Llanfair Caereinion

No. 822 at Llanfair Caereinion station on 10th September 1951. The goods stock at this date comprised two brake vans, four goods vans, two cattle vans, six open sheep trucks, thirty-one opens, and four timber trucks, all of W&LLR/Cambrian origin; two cattle vans and four opens built by the GWR-built and six smaller opens converted by the GWR from timber trucks. The two GWR-built cattle vans were originally built in 1923 for the Vale of Rheidol before being regauged and transferred to the W&L in 1937. The cattle van on the far right is one of the former VoR vans. Unlike the other Welsh narrow gauge railways there were no slate quarries on the line generating outgoing mineral revenue, so the traffic along the line consisted of mixed merchandise, coal for local consumption and livestock for the cattle market. All but the latter required labour intensive transhipment at Welshpool, so it was surprising the line lasted until 1956. The terminus at Llanfair Caereinion had a combined booking office and waiting room and a goods shed, cattle dock, loop and originally two sidings, soon increased to cater for the timber traffic. The galvanised store shed on the left of the train was added in 1938.

Rail Archive Stephenson

Seven Stars

Above: No. 822 threads it way through the town at the site of the former Seven Stars halt, which took its name from the nearby public house, as it approaches the Church Street crossing with a special excursion organised by the Locomotive Club of Great Britain on 23rd June 1956. Platform seats from the main line station were placed on the open wagons and, before setting off, the stationmaster collected from the passengers signed statements that they would not claim damages from British Railways if they came to any harm.

Right: This 1965 picture taken a short distance nearer to Church Street than the previous one, in the now demolished 'Narrows', shows the longitudinal timbering either side of the rails supported by steel cross girders – at this point the railway was on a continuous bridge over the Lledan Brook. After Church Street it crossed over the Shropshire Union Canal before it reached the terminus alongside the Cambrian Railways' station.

13 – Welshpool to Oswestry

The Oswestry & Newtown Railway opened the line between Oswestry and Welshpool in August 1860 and on to Newtown in June 1861. The three miles from Buttington to Welshpool was built as a single track but before it was completed the London & North Western Railway reached an agreement to use the line and the right for access to Welshpool station. This enabled the Shrewsbury & Welshpool Railway, which was operated by the L&NWR, to complete its route from Shrewsbury through to Welshpool. As part of this arrangement the Oswestry & Newtown agreed to convert the Buttington-Welshpool section to double track and this was opened in January 1863. Also in 1863, the Oswestry & Newtown Railway opened an 8½ mile long branch from the station at Llanymynech to Llanfyllin.

In 1864 the Oswestry & Newtown Railway amalgamated with the Newtown & Llandiloes Railway, the Oswestry Ellesmere & Whitchurch Railway and the Newtown & Machynlleth Railway to form the Cambrian Railways. The end in 1865 of what had been a complex series of negotiations saw the Shrewsbury & Welshpool Railway become a joint line, owned equally by the GWR and the L&NWR.

On 18th January 1965 the line between Buttington and Llynclys Junction closed completely; trains ran between Shrewsbury and Aberystwyth via the Joint line from Buttington to Welshpool.

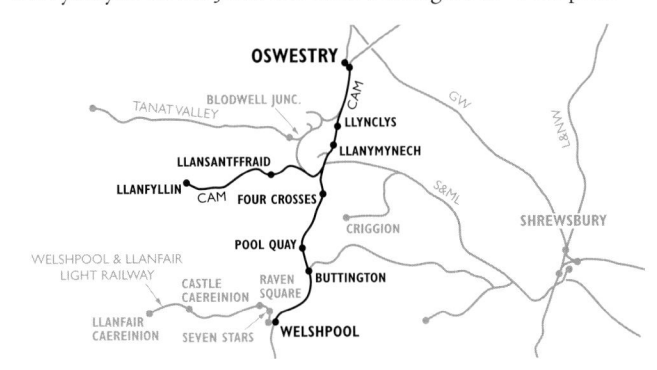

Buttington

No. 7821 *Ditcheat Manor* near Buttington on an Aberystwyth-Whitchurch local in around 1963. Following withdrawal from Shrewsbury in November 1965, it went to Woodhams' scrapyard at Barry from where it was purchased for preservation in 1981. After it was restored to working order in 1998, No. 7821 ran on several preserved railways until its boiler ticket expired. It is now owned by the West Somerset Railway Association and is currently on loan to the McArthur Glen Designer Outlet in Swindon until funds can be raised for a major overhaul.

BR Standard Class '4' 4-6-0 No. 75002 on an Up train at Buttington in 1964. It had been on the Cambrian for three months at the end of 1956 allocated to Oswestry and returned to the line at Machynlleth in 1962; it was in lined green from November 1957. On the right is the Grade II listed Buttington Bridge on the Shrewsbury-Welshpool road which is still in use today. Built in 1872, the single span bridge was chosen because it was '*an interesting late use of cast iron in prefabricated sections to provide a worthy major river bridge*'.

The level crossing of the Shrewsbury-Welshpool road by the signal box on the left remains an operational problem even today with accidents still being reported. It was formerly controlled by a compact Dutton & Co. signal box, known as Buttington Gates which was replaced in April 1962 by Buttington Crossing signal box, although the old crossing gates were retained. This was a BR (Western Region) standard 'Type 37B' box of all timber construction but within just five years was reduced to a 'gate box' in October 1967 when the line from Buttington Crossing to Welshpool was singled. Cross Newydd's BR Standard Class '4' 4-6-0 No. 75009 has just passed the crossing with a northbound train in 1964. Unlike most of the other Western Region Class '4' engines it was not repainted in green livery at Swindon.

No. 7802 *Bradley Manor* at Buttington Crossing double-heading with No. 7812 *Erlestoke Manor* on the Talyllyn Railway Preservation Society A.G.M. Special to Towyn on 25th September 1965. The two 'Manors' took over the train which No. 4079 *Pendennis Castle* had brought from Paddington to Shrewsbury. The following day, the pair returned the party to Shrewsbury where a Brush Type '4' took the special to Tyseley before No. 4079 came on for the return to London. Both 'Manors' are preserved and based at the Severn Valley Railway having been rescued from Barry Docks.

CHAPTER 13 - WELSHPOOL TO OSWESTRY

Four Crosses

The line was single track north of Buttington, and Four Crosses originally had one platform with a brick-built two-storey station building. Goods facilities were south of the station with a large brick-built, single-road goods shed. During the 1890s the Cambrian Railways made improvements along the line and at Four Crosses station a passing loop and a new platform were opened in July 1899. The platform had to be located to the south of the original opposite the goods shed and a barrow crossing linked the south end of the Up platform to the north end of the Down. Four Crosses was mentioned in the 1963 comedic song 'The Slow Train' by Michael Flanders and Donald Swann. This was about the railways which would soon be lost under rationalisation and was first performed as part of their musical revue 'At the Drop of Another Hat'; it included many other stations that were earmarked for closure in the Beeching Report.

Now preserved No. 7822 *Foxcote Manor* on a Welshpool to Whitchurch local in around 1962. The Down platform on the left, added when the station was enlarged, had a small timber-built, single-storey waiting room which is just visible behind the signal box and is on the right in the picture of No. 80070 below.

BR Standard Class '4' 2-6-4T No. 80070 on a southbound local at Four Crosses in 1963. It was originally on the London, Tilbury & Southend line until July 1962 when it was displaced by electrification and moved to Old Oak Common, then on to Shrewsbury in November. Apart from a short spell at Croes Newydd in early 1963 it stayed there until April 1965 when it went to Eastleigh. The large building in the background was a creamery which specialised in cheese production and bulk liquid milk distribution; it closed in 1992.

On 30th March 1964, an Ivatt Class '2' 2-6-0 sets off from Four Crosses with the 4.30pm from Whitchurch to Welshpool. The provision of First Class accommodation amounting to a quarter of the train seems rather excessive for a local service. The first coach is passing over the barrow crossing which linked the south end of the Up platform to the north end of the Down platform. The main station building was an attractive brick-built villa of two storeys. The signal box could be 'switched out' here, trains using the 'Up' line in both directions.

Llanymynech

Llanymynech station was opened by the Oswestry & Newtown Railway in 1860 on the single line between Oswestry and Welshpool. In July 1863 the Railway opened a branch line from Llanymynech to Llanfyllin which had its own bay platform at the north end of the station. During the second half of 1863 work began to double the line between Oswestry and Llanymynech and this was completed in February 1864.

Croes Newydd's No. 7828 *Odney Manor* arriving at Llanymynech on a local train to Oswestry on 24th October 1962. From July 1956 Swindon began repainting the 'Manor' class in lined green and No. 7828 was the first to return to traffic in this livery. The main timber-built station building on the Up platform dated from around the time the line was doubled.

The Ivatt Class '2' 2-6-0s worked on the Llanfyllin branch up to its closure in January 1965. They usually ran tender-first from Oswestry towards Llanfyllin as illustrated by No. 46509 at Llanymynech with the branch 'B'-set on 15th June 1962. The running-in board stated 'LLANYMYNECH CHANGE FOR LLANFYLLIN BRANCH AND LAKE VYRNWY'. The latter was a five miles long reservoir completed in 1889 to supply Liverpool with water via a 75-mile long aqueduct; it was the first large stone-built dam in Britain. On the left is the Llanfyllin bay platform, rendered superfluous by the alterations made in 1896 to allow access to the branch south of the station. In the background the original route for the branch is still just about visible. The overgrown sidings curving away to the right of the station behind the sign 'W.D. LAND ENTRY PROHIBITED' are the remains of the short-lived Potteries, Shrewsbury & North Wales Railway line from Shrewsbury opened in 1866; the P.S.& N.W. also built a 3¾ mile long branch from Llanymynech to Nantmawr. The line was not a success and the company soon went into receivership; the Nantmawr branch continued in use for mineral trains which were operated by the Cambrian Railways. Colonel Holman F. Stephens took an interest in the derelict line, referred to locally as 'The Potts'. He obtained a Light Railway Order and rebuilt it in typical fashion using the original infrastructure where possible. The line from Shrewsbury to Llanymynech was reopened as the Shropshire & Montgomeryshire Light Railway in April 1911. Bus competition saw off the daily passenger services in 1933 and by 1940 closure seemed inevitable. However, the line was taken over by the Army to serve a network of munitions stores and it continued in Army use until 1960, hence the sign.

The man and child on the Down platform watch a sight which was soon to disappear for good. Ivatt Class '2' 2-6-0 No. 46509 was working the 12.55pm to Llanfyllin in January 1965, the final month of operation.

K.L. Cook/Rail Archive Stephenson

The Llanfyllin branch

On 11th July 1863 the Oswestry & Newtown Railway opened an 8½ mile long line from Llanymynech to Llanfyllin. The Llanfyllin branch had its junction with the main line 15 chains north of the station and it faced northwards. Trains from Oswestry arriving in the branch bay platform therefore had to be propelled from the bay platform out to a headshunt at the junction where the train would then reverse before the engine hauled it to Llanfyllin; the move had to be performed in reverse for arriving branch line trains. However, in 1896 this was eliminated by construction of a short, half mile-long spur from the branch to the line from Llanymynech to Nantmawr which started to the south of the station.

The GWR invested in the branch in 1933 when a brand new '58XX' 0-4-2T was allocated to Llanfyllin shed and steel panelled, close-coupled 'B'-sets with electric lighting replaced the old Cambrian coaching stock. The 0-4-2Ts would dominate the passenger trains until 1953 when Ivatt Class '2' 2-6-0s took over; their BR Standard equivalents also made a brief appearance until they were transferred away from Oswestry. '74XX' pannier tanks took over freight duties from 'Dean Goods' 0-6-0s in the late 1940s. Both the Ivatts and the 'B'-sets remained in use until closure in January 1965. There was a permanent speed restriction of 30mph on the branch.

Llansantffraid

The strawberries are flowering on the trackside allotment as Ivatt Class '2' 2-6-0 No. 46518 approaches Llansantffraid with a train from Oswestry on 30th May 1963. Some of the branch trains ran beyond Oswestry to Gobowen and apparently the clearance between the buffer stops and the end of the bay platform there was insufficient if the engine was arriving tender-first and hence the engines would face northwards when running the branch service. The tender cabs of the 2-6-0s ensured that tender-first working was not an unpleasant change for the footplatemen who had become used to their enclosed tank engine cabs.

Ivatt Class '2' 2-6-0 No. 46512 with a train to Oswestry at Llansantffraid, which was the principal intermediate station and the only crossing point on the branch, in the early 1960s. 46512 was built at Swindon in December 1952 and was allocated to Oswestry until the shed closed in January 1965. The station included a two-storey home with a bay window facing the platform for the stationmaster and his family.

Llanfyllin

Viewed from the bufferstops, an unidentified 2-6-0 has arrived at Llanfyllin on a winter's day in the early 1960s. It is ready to uncouple and run around its train to return to Oswestry. There was no turntable at the terminus, hence the 2-6-0s usually ran tender-first down the branch as described on the previous page; the small engine shed at Llanfyllin was closed in 1952. There is at least one recorded instance of a 2-6-0, BR Standard No. 78005 in 1953, working on the branch facing in the opposite direction.

A regular engine on the branch, Ivatt Class '2' 2-6-0 No. 46512 is about to run round its coaches at Llanfyllin before leaving as the 4.5pm school train to Llanymynech and Oswestry in September 1964. The scheduled journey time from Llanfyllin to Llanymynech was twenty-four minutes but in the other direction it was twenty-five minutes.

J. Suter / I. Travers

Llynclys

'2251' 0-6-0 No. 2255 on the 10.20am Welshpool-Whitchurch passing Haystack Siding Ground Frame as it approaches Llynclys on the double track section of the Cambrian main line in the early 1950s. It was the fifth of the class when built in March 1930 and had been allocated to Oswestry since before nationalisation. No. 2255 was transferred to Machynlleth in July 1955 and was withdrawn from there in May 1962.

Ivatt Class '2' 2-6-0 No. 46512 arriving at Llynclys with the usual two coach train from Llanfyllin to Oswestry on 2nd November 1964. When the axe fell on the lines worked by the Oswestry Ivatts and the shed closed in January 1965, No. 46512 was transferred on loan to Shrewsbury before moving on to Willesden two weeks later. After it was withdrawn in November 1966 No. 46512 was sold for scrap to Woodham Brothers at Barry, staying there until 1973 when it was purchased by the embryonic Strathspey Railway for its Aviemore to Boat of Garten line. It was stored on the Severn Valley Railway before moving up to the Strathspey Railway in 1982 to begin restoration, which was completed in 2000. No. 46512 worked until 2005 and then underwent a major overhaul which took around six years. Its boiler was re-tubed and cylinders re-bored in late 2017 and No. 46512 returned to traffic in early 2018.

BR Standard Class '4' 2-6-4T No. 80070 pulls into Llynclys with a southbound train. It had been on the London, Tilbury & Southend until July 1962 and moved at Shrewsbury in November 1962. Apart from a short spell at Croes Newydd in early 1963 it stayed there until April 1965. In the distance on the left is Llynclys Junction signal box where in May 1861 a short branch was opened to serve the quarries at Porthywaen.

14 – Oswestry

In 1860 the Oswestry & Newtown Railway opened its Oswestry station on the eastern edge of the town next to the Great Western Railway station which been in use since 1849. It was the principal station of the company and in 1862 the O&NR moved its headquarters there from Welshpool. Work commenced in 1863 on a large station building that would also house the headquarters, located on the Up platform to the south of the original building. It was a massive structure, particularly in relation to the size of the town and had twenty bays with two tall storeys and a hipped roof; an awning ran the whole length of the building on the platform side.

The GWR station was closed within a year of the 1923 Grouping since the amalgamated company did not need two stations in the town, especially since they were so close together. The Cambrian Railways facility was the obvious choice to concentrate all of the traffic there. This was facilitated by using a connection between the GWR's Gobowen branch and its Ellesmere line, and the Cambrian station was extended at the north end and a bay platform constructed for the Gobowen trains. This enabled the GWR station to be closed to passengers on 7th July 1924 when it was handed over to the goods department and it remained in use as a goods station until December 1971.

The Cambrian station was closed to passengers in November 1966. The Down platform building was demolished in 1972 and in the following years the Up station building/offices fell into a state of dereliction. In 2005 it was purchased by Oswestry Borough Council who renovated it, creating a restaurant and visitor centre on the ground floor with offices on the first floor. The building was subsequently leased to the Oswestry Station Building Trust.

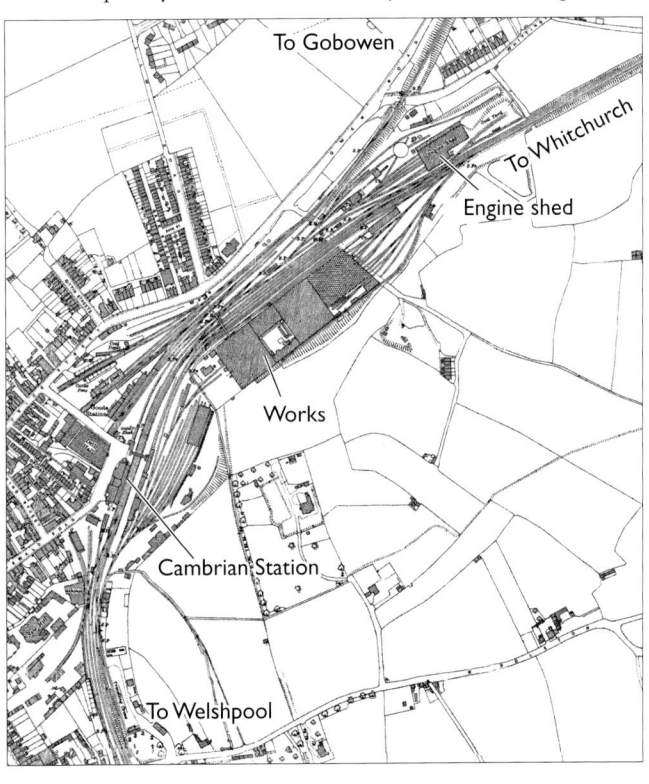

Stations

From an age when young ladies still cycled to and from work even in winter and army officers walked along the pavements ignoring trains, a '14XX' 0-4-2T with a two-coach Auto-Train heads away from Oswestry towards Gobowen on the 2½ mile long journey which took eight minutes. The train is about to pass over the Vyrnwy aqueduct that feeds Liverpool with water from Lake Vyrnwy.

There is plenty of activity on the platform as '14XX' No. 1458 waits to depart to Gobowen. Three or four Collett 0-4-2Ts were allocated to Oswestry up until 1963 primarily for the services on the Wrexham to Ellesmere and Gobowen branches. No. 1458 has an 89D shed plate, dating this photograph after 1st January 1961 when the shed code was changed from 89A. It was fitted with a top feed boiler in 1961 only to lose it again by 1963.

The Auto-Train service originally ran into the GWR station which was just off to the right of this picture. When this was closed in July 1924 the Gobowen shuttle trains used the new bay platform in which No. 1458 is standing which was added to the Cambrian Railways station.

The north elevation of the main station building cum Cambrian Railways' headquarters towers above the platform in the left background.

'2251' 0-6-0 No. 2294 working a Down stopper to Welshpool tops up its tender water tank in the late 1950s. Built in February 1938, this picture was taken after it had been transferred to Machynlleth in October 1959. No. 2294 had spent most of the 1950s in Wales, at both Wrexham sheds, Rhosddu and Croes Newydd, and also at Oswestry although mostly in store there. It was withdrawn from Machynlleth in September 1962. Oswestry shed had four '2251's at nationalisation and this increased a decade later to nine but by late 1962 had dropped back to three. Behind the train is the Down station building which dated from 1893 when the Cambrian Railways added a platform to the east of the original. This became the Down platform and the original became the Up platform. Additional facilities were provided in a building whose exterior design complemented that of the 1863 structure opposite.

CHAPTER 14 - OSWESTRY

A nice overhead view of '16xx' 0-6-0PT No. 1636 at the north end of Oswestry station in 1961 showing the flat casing over the smokebox with the chimney base set in. On the left is the end wall of Oswestry Works and on the right a '14XX' 0-4-2T simmers in the Gobowen bay. No. 1636 went new to Oswestry in March 1951, moving to Machynlleth in February 1954 and returning to Oswestry in August 1959. It left there for its final posting to Slough in August 1962 and was withdrawn in June 1964.

Below: No. 1636 has just passed in front of Oswestry North signal box (on the extreme left of the photograph) with a short train of 'Conflat L' container wagons carrying limestone. It has an 89A shed plate which dates the picture to before January 1961 when Oswestry shed was recoded to 89D. The roof of the weighbridge office has seen better days and drivers were advised by the sign that they must not exceed 4 m.p.h. when passing over the weighbridge.

Ivatt Class '2' 2-6-0 No. 46510 at Oswestry with a southbound train in the early 1960s. It was allocated to Oswestry until the shed closed in January 1965 moving to Shrewsbury for its last few months in service. The Down platform had a short umbrella canopy supported on cast iron pillars.

BR Standard Class '4' 2-6-4T No. 80135 arriving at Oswestry in 1963, probably on a local service from Shrewsbury to Aberystwyth. Originally on the London, Tilbury & Southend line it moved to Shrewsbury in 1962, then on to Oswestry in January 1963 before returning to Shrewsbury in September 1964. It was bought from Woodham Brothers scrapyard at Barry Docks by the North Yorkshire Moors Railway in 1973 and following restoration has been used on that line since then. The large building in the right background is Oswestry Works. The long footbridge visible under the signal gantry connected Gobowen Road to the Works and provided a short-cut from the town.

BR Standard Class '2' 2-6-2T No. 84004 Oswestry on the Gobowen service. With No. 84000 from Warrington Dallam, it was transferred to Oswestry from Bletchley in April 1963 and they took over the Gobowen shuttle from the '14XX' 0-4-2Ts with their GWR auto-coaches in July; both stayed until the shed closed in January 1965 when they moved to Croes Newydd.

An unidentified BR Standard Class '2' 2-6-0 passes southbound through the station with a long train of open wagons in late 1965 or early 1966. The Up platform had a short awning of ridged profile that did not stretch the full length of the station building, unlike that on the opposite platform.

Another unidentified BR Standard Class '2' 2-6-0 shunts in the goods yard in front of the former GWR station building and a two-car Metro-Cammell DMU is in the bay platform on the Gobowen shuttle. The goods yard is surprisingly busy at this late date, probably 1965, and would remain in use for another six years until 1971.

Two Ivatt Class '2' 2-6-0s, Nos.46510 and 46511, running tender-first on a heavy train including stone in 'Mermaid' ballast wagons from Llynclys to Gobowen in August 1965. The engine shed is in the background above the two engines, the Works is on the right and Oswestry North signal box is visible above the DMU.

A Metro-Cammell two-car DMU, which became Class '111' under TOPS, waits in the Gobowen bay at a virtually deserted Oswestry in 1965. The introduction of the diesel units increased the shuttle service to twenty-one trains daily in each direction. The size of the station building which incorporated the Cambrian's headquarters dwarfs that of the building on the Down platform.

A Derby two-car DMU departing from Oswestry for Gobowen in August 1965. This was built in 1959 becoming Class '108' under TOPS. A batch were allocated to Wrexham from new and were subsequently transferred to Chester which already had a number of these sets. For some reason, the Oswestry-Gobowen line was not mentioned in the 1963 Beeching Report and the service continued until November 1966, nearly two years after the passenger service on the main line between Whitchurch and Welshpool had been withdrawn.

Oswestry shed

Oswestry, the largest locomotive depot on the Cambrian Railways, was opened in 1860 by the Oswestry & Newtown Railway as a four-road, dead-ended 200ft long shed, which was extended in the early twentieth century with the addition of a shorter two-road building, 125ft long. In the 1920s the GWR modernised the depot by adding electric lighting, additional inspection pits, a standard single-ramp coaling stage and a 45,000-gallon water tank; a new, hand-operated, 65ft diameter turntable replaced the original 45ft one. In 1949/50 the wooden roof was replaced with steel trusses, allowing the introduction of improved clearances, increased ventilation and additional glass shuttering.

In 1950 its allocation comprised eight Cambrian Railways Class '15' 0-6-0s, fourteen 'Dean Goods' 0-6-0s, three Collett '2251' 0-6-0s, three 'Manor' 4-6-0s, seven '90XX' 4-4-0s and one 'Duke' 4-4-0, seven '14XX/58XX' 0-4-2Ts, four '2021' 0-6-0PTs, one '16XX' and three '74XX' 0-6-0PTs and a single '81XX' 2-6-2T. A decade later, the Ivatt 2-6-0s had swept away the older 0-6-0s numbering twenty-four, with nine pannier tanks, seven 'Manor' 4-6-0s, five '2251' 0-6-0s, and single examples of '90XX' 4-4-0s, '14XX' 0-4-2Ts, '43XX' 2-6-0s and Ivatt 2-6-2Ts.

At nationalisation Oswestry was coded 89A and at the end of 1960 it was re-coded to 89D. In September 1963 when it became part of the London Midland Region it became 6E, a sub shed of Chester, which continued until it was closed in January 1965 at which date most of its allocation was transferred to either Croes Newydd or Shrewsbury. It originally had five sub-sheds: Llanfyllin (closed in 1952), Llanidloes (closed in 1962), Moat Lane (closed in December 1962), Welshpool & Llanfair narrow gauge (closed in November 1956), and Whitchurch (closed in September 1957).

Oswestry shed on 4th June 1960 with, on the left, the original but heavily rebuilt four-road building, opened by the Oswestry and Newtown Railway in 1866, and on the right the smaller two-road addition on the right added some years later by the Cambrian Railways. Great Western classes predominate including several 'Manor' 4-6-0s and a '2251' 0-6-0 although at least a couple of the large allocation of Ivatt 2-6-0s are inside. The standard GWR single-ramp coaling stage topped by a 45,000-gallon water tank was installed in 1929.

A lightweight version of the ubiquitous GWR pannier tank, '16XX' 0-6-0PT No. 1604 at Oswestry shed on 26th February 1950. Along with Nos.1603 and 1605, 1604 was stored for nearly three months when built at the end of 1949 before arriving at Oswestry in January 1950 where it would remain for the next decade until taken out of service in July 1960. The vehicle behind the pannier is a GWR Permanent Way brake van, effectively a 'Toad' with its veranda enclosed built to either diagram AA6, or perhaps the unique vehicle of diagram AA14.

A very clean ex-works Cambrian Railways Class '15' 0-6-0 No. 895 on shed in September 1949. It was one of five built by Beyer, Peacock & Co. in 1908 and one of eleven on the shed's allocation at nationalisation. No. 895, and also No. 894, had been fitted with narrow rectangular cab front windows whereas the other Beyer, Peacock built Class '15's had small circular ones. It was one of the last three remaining Cambrian Railways' engines when withdrawn in October 1954, together with the other two survivors, Nos. 849 and 855. No. 895 and No. 849 were both reported working passenger trains at Barmouth as late as July 1954, although they were normally on freight duties.

Cambrian Railways Class '15' 0-6-0 No. 855 parked up at Oswestry with a full tender of coal in the early 1950s was one of five built by Beyer, Peacock & Co. in 1918/19. Note the difference in the front cab windows from No. 895 above; the latter had been fitted with narrow rectangular whereas other Beyer, Peacock engines had small circular ones. The large vacuum pipe running along the boiler indicates that it had been fitted with large and small ejectors whereas No. 895 had a large ejector and crosshead vacuum pump.

'Dean Goods' 0-6-0 No. 2323 was transferred to Oswestry from Machynlleth in April 1953, ousted by the arrival of new BR Standard and Ivatt Class '2' 2-6-0s but was withdrawn from Oswestry two months later. It was one of the second batch of the class and was built in 1884. Forty-seven of these engines were allocated to Central Wales sheds immediately before the Second World War but this had reduced to twenty-one by 1947 following the requisition of a hundred by the War Department for overseas use and which were never returned to GWR stock.

'14XX' 0-4-2T No. 1459 outside the original four-road shed at Oswestry was allocated there for the push-pull service to Gobowen, one of four of the 0-4-2Ts on its books in the early 1950s. The BR Standard Class '2' 2-6-0 No. 78002 in the background was one of the first ten of the class which went initially to Oswestry when they emerged from Darlington Works in late 1952 and early 1953. Their predecessors, the LM&SR Ivatt 2-6-0s, were also on Oswestry's allocation and No. 46510 on the right was there until 1965 but No. 78002 left for Machynlleth in May 1953, thus dating this picture as early 1953.

Shunting the Loco Coal wagons at Oswestry on 21st July 1964, '16XX' 0-6-0PT No. 1632. Built by British Railways in January 1951, it had moved to Oswestry in May 1962 after spending its early years at Lydney but was only there for a couple of months, ending its days at Croes Newydd until withdrawal in April 1965. However, it returned on loan to Oswestry in June 1964 for several months.

Oswestry Works

After the Cambrian Railways had moved its headquarters to Oswestry it built a locomotive, carriage and wagon works there in 1866 on a site to the north of the station. It was housed in a single 812ft by 210ft building. The locomotive erecting shop had a hand-operated central traverser which served twelve roads on each side. Apart from the entrance and exit roads, each of the other roads could accommodate a single locomotive or other piece of rolling stock. Although many carriages and wagons were built in the workshops, only two locomotives were ever built there.

Following the 1923 Grouping, the Great Western kept the works open as a regional carriage and wagon works, and locomotive repair shop although engines which needed a heavy overhaul and a boiler lift went either to Wolverhampton or Swindon. A phased shutdown began in 1964 which ended with the closing of the locomotive repair shops on 31st December 1966, the last former GWR works to overhaul steam locomotives.

The Works was given Grade II listing in 1986 for its historical significance and architectural merits. An antiques centre, small business hub and document storage centre have since been located there. In July 2011, after extensive renovation to the southern section of the buildings, Oswestry Health Centre opened on the works site as a multi-purpose outpatient healthcare centre.

The engines from the Welshpool and Llanfair Light Railway were maintained at the Works. No. 823 was sent there for storage in March 1956 when it was deemed unserviceable, and was joined in May 1958 by No. 822, eighteen months after the line closed. This picture was taken on 4th June 1960 with No. 823 in the foreground and No. 822 in the background. No. 823 was the first to be restored, in 1961 after it had been purchased by the Preservation Society from British Railways. No. 823 followed suit after completion of heavy repairs in October 1962.

Oliver Veltom, the Oswestry District Traffic Superintendent, who had already safeguarded the survival of the two Welshpool & Llanfair locomotives from the scrap man by keeping them in the Works, had placed the last '90XX' 4-4-0 No. 9017 in store there following its withdrawal in October 1960, to allow time for the funds for its preservation to be raised. No. 9017 left the Works in February 1962 for the Bluebell Railway where it has been based ever since; in 2009 it visited the Llangollen Railway.

Left: '16XX' 0-6-0PT No. 1632 and an unidentified BR Standard 2-6-4T in the Works showing the traverser down the centre of the Erecting Shop and the short roads on either side. The 6C Croes Newydd shed plate on No. 1632 dates the picture as post-September 1963. Although most of the locomotives repaired there were the local 0-6-0s, 2-6-0s and tank engines, the Works even carried out minor repairs on larger engines such as '9F' 2-10-0s; a Stanier 'Jubilee', No. 45572 *Eire* from Shrewsbury, was noted there in August 1963.